Television and Film

An Annotated Bibliography of Research Materials

Frank W. Hoffmann

Editor: Richard J. Wood

Paw Paw Press

2015

Family Watching Television in the 1950s

TABLE OF CONTENTS

INTRODUCTION   5

Almanacs--Television   8
Anthologies--Film Industry   8
Associations and Societies--Film Industry   9
Associations and Societies—Television   12
Atlases--Television   16
Bibliographies/Filmographies/Videographies   17
Bibliographies--Television   21
Biographical Sources –Film Industry   23
Biographical Sources--Television   34
Biographies/Career Retrospective--Film Industry   38
Catalogs/Union Lists--Film Industry   63
Catalogs/Union List--Television   63
Cellector and Price Guides--Television   64
Dictionaries--Film Industry   66
Dictionaries--Television   67
Directories--Film Industry   68
Directories--Television   69
Encyclopedia--Film Industry   69
Encyclopedias--Television   72
Guides to the Literature--Television   75
Handbooks--Film Industry   75
Handbooks--Television   109
Indexes--Film Industry   131
Indexas--Television   135
Journals--General   136
Journals--Film Industry   136
Journals--Television   139
Manuals--Film Industry   140
Manuals--Television   140
Special Collections--Film Industry   148
Special Collections--Television   150
Yearbooks and Annuals--Television   151

Casablanca film still

INTRODUCTION

The Popular Culture Dilemma

Those of us involved within the educational sector - whether as teachers, scholars and investigators, library/information specialists, or students - find ourselves overwhelmed by the wealth of resources available to the public dealing with television and the cinema, particularly the American scene. The mass media - which now includes electronic publications available via the Internet, list serves, e-mail, etc. - pumps out literature on these, and other popular culture subjects, at a prolific rate. Much of it is of questionable value, featuring bad writing, factual inaccuracies, biases, and pointless trivia. However, some of this material provides valuable insights into the development and appeal of contemporary TV and film. Therefore, it is imperative that we exercise insight and objectivity in selecting such resources for use in classrooms and libraries.

Carrying out the evaluation and selection function requires continued commitment underscored by resourcefulness and vigilance. The overwhelming abundance of titles to choose from promotes a false sense of security on the part of teachers and librarians; with so many popular resources available, it is hard to envision any kind of problem with regard to the acquisition process. However, many of these materials - whether in print, electronic, or multimedia formats - are exceedingly hard to obtain. They are not marketed through traditional educational channels and are rarely noted by widely respected review sources. If not acquired as quickly as possible once they become available through the marketplace, many of these items disappear for good. In addition to a strong underlying motivation (e.g., cultural elitism, offense taken at the demonstration of politically incorrect attitudes), educators tend to lack the background knowledge necessary to separate the wheat from the chaff regarding pop resources. The prior record exhibited by educators is not an encouraging one. In recent years teachers (who, in truth, deserve only partial blame) seem to have been preoccupied with preparing students to pass government-sponsored standardized tests, while librarians - long an irrelevant force to many citizens - are caught up in trying to ascertain their particular role within the automation revolution.

In view of their central role in providing learning resources and information for teachers, students, and the community at large, librarians and media specialists represent a particularly vital cog in any attempt to change perceptions toward popular resources within the educational sector. As far back as 1970, Don Roberts recognized both the importance - and relative failure - of librarians to take a leadership role regarding the acquisition and use of these materials:

We have a negative commitment to the popular culture of our society,
even though this culture (especially in the music industry) is of the highest
it has been for many, many generations. The shocking, repetitious print
equivalent stuff pouring out of the publishing houses is reviewed, purchased,
and processed toward oblivion on the shelves regardless, while the Number

One recorded literature is not even considered! And so we continue to run the vestiges of a defunct Western humanism and post-Renaissance classicism (typified in a way by the Caldecott/Newbery awards and book selection mystiques) on the hapless, cynical library dropout taxpayers and their children. (1)

Over the years, many other librarians and educators have echoed Roberts' call to action, including Ray Browne (2), Gordon Stevenson, Carlos Hagen, B. Lee Cooper, William Schurk, Haynes McMullen, Jay Dailey, Allen Ellis, and Marshall Fishwick. The present work falls within this tradition in its attempt to compile - and discuss - those research materials likely to be of value to educators, students, and other individuals interested in background information on television and motion pictures.

Television and Film Coverage by the Traditional Literature

Despite the spotty record on the part of educators in utilizing popular culture resources, there exist a significant number of titles--including traditional reference categories such as biographical sources, encyclopedias, handbooks, etc.--possessing inherent research value. Even those tools geared primarily to casual reading by a lay audience which were once available primarily through mail order firms and retail stores, are now found in libraries to an increasingly greater degree.

The resources comprising *Television and Film: An Annotated Bibliography of Research Materials* have been culled from essentially the same sources a searcher might employ in accessing a wide range of present-day topics, most notably catalogs and union lists of library holdings (many of which are now available online). While certain high-profile guides to the reference literature offered poor coverage, other tools provided a wealth of useful entries, most notably regularly updated retrospective guides to the literature, Internet retail sites, commercial bibliographies, periodical indexes, and current review journals (encompassing professional, trade, scholarly, and mass circulation titles). Libraries of all types presently include these lead-in tools in their respective collections as well as some of the information sources documenting television and the cinema found within this work.

The increasing attention being given popular culture materials by educators renders it likely that the television and film literature will find greater representation within library collections. Until that void is more adequately filled, however, this work will serve to assist librarians, educators, students, researchers, and other enthusiasts in identifying those sources that delineate notable television and film topics with the greatest degree of thoroughness, authoritativeness, timeliness and accuracy.

Abbreviations

bibl. bibliography
comp. compiler
ed. edition

il. illustrations
n.d. no date
p. pages
pap. paperback

Notes

(1) Don Roberts. "Listen, Miss, Mrs., Mr. Librarian," *Library Journal.* (November 15, 1970) 30.

(2) Ray Browne is widely recognized as the foremost pioneer in elevating popular culture to the status of an academic discipline. The institution where he has been affiliated for over four decades, Bowling Green State University, has offered a Ph.D in American Culture/Popular Culture since the late 1960s. His perceptions of the field are clearly outlined in the Introduction to his landmark work, *Popular Culture and the Expanding Consciousness* (New York: Wiley, 1973).

ALMANACS--TELEVISION

Phillips, Louis, and Burnham Holmes. The TV Almanac. New York: Macmillan, 1994. 276p. il. index. ISBN 0-671-88798-X.
A concise factual compendium concerned with all facets of the television industry. The topical breakdowns include: Opening Lines of Classic TV Shows; Inside Television (viewing habits, rating, TV jargon); A Brief TV History (including a chronology and notable TV first--e.g., the first color transmission, New York skyline, 1945); The Shows; Some TV Lists (e.g., TV animals, famous wheels, addresses of TV characters); The Awards (Emmys, Golden Globes); A TV Who's Who (TV title roles, TV celebrities AZ); The Fans (fan clubs, TV museums); and Famous Sign-offs.

ANTHOLOGIES--FILM INDUSTRY

Lucas, Tim. The Video Watchdog Book. Cincinnati, OH: Video Watchdog, 1992. 391p. $19.95 pap. ISBN 0-9633756-0-1.
A fascinating compilation of articles written by Tim Lucas for various publications as well as his own magazine *Video Watchdog*, this volume brings these works together and includes a fine variety of illustrated material. Reprinted and updated are Lucas' pieces for such publications as Video Times, Overview, Gorezone, Fangoria, and Film Comment. In addition to addressing various movies regarding such things as censored scenes, alternate versions and retitles, the author also does several in-depth studies, the most interesting on the films of Jess Franco and Edgar Wallace. There is a very useful sectio n on video retitles and two indexes, one for the book and one for the first twelve issues of Lucas' magazine.

Maltin, Leonard, ed. Hollywood: The Movie Factory. York: Popular Library, 1976. 284p. $1.50 pap.
Consists of reprints of articles originally published in Leonard Maltin's *Film Fan Monthly* magazine. Mostly celebrity interviews and career articles, the book's subjects include Ralph Bellamy, Joan Blondell, Johnny Mack Brown, Henry Wilcoxon, Elliott Nugent, Anita Loos, and Burgess Meredith. Other articles include the Hollywood Studio Club, the Torchy Blane series, Tom & Jerry cartoons and a review of some vintage MGM features.

Slide, Anthony. The Best of Rob Wagner's Script. Metuchen, NJ: Scarecrow Press, 1985. 183p. $15.00. ISBN 0-8108-1810-8.
A compilation of articles from the Beverly Hills, California, based magazine Rob Wagner's *Script* make up this small volume which is mainly of interest due to its writers. They include

Charles Chaplin, William Saroyan, Ray Bradbury, Jessamyn West, Upton Sinclair, Sigmund Romberg, Eddie Cantor, Agnes De Mille, Ben Hecht, Herb Sterne, Irving Wallace, Dore Schary, Lillian Gish, and Louis L'Amour. One amusing poem by Gene Lockhart uses James Whitcomb Riley's work "Little Orphant Annie" to poke fun at Orson Welles.

Spears, Jack. Hollywood: The Golden Era. New York: Castle Books, 1971. 440p. $10.00.
A series of articles which first appeared in *Films in Review* are included in book form, all written by noted film historian Jack Spears. The thoroughly researched and very informative pieces include a comprehensive study of World War I films, the careers of Max Linder, Norma Talmadge, and Colleen Moore, directors Marshal Neilan and Robert Florey, baseball on film, the collaborators of Charles Chaplin, screen comic strips, and movies about doctors and Native Americans. With thorough name and film title indexes, the book is an important contribution to cinema literature.

ASSOCIATIONS AND SOCIETIES--FILM INDUSTRY

Academy of Family Films and Family Television. c/o Dr. Donald A. Reed, Director. 334 W. 54th St., Los Angeles, CA 90037. (213) 752-5811.
The academy, founded in 1980, is comprised of individuals and groups devoted to promoting the arts and sciences of family entertainment. Opposed in principle to censorship, it presents annual recognition awards, holds screenings of recommended programs, and publishes a quarterly newsletter.

Academy of Science Fiction, Fantasy, and Horror Films. c/o Dr. Donald A. Reed, President. 334 W. 54th St., Los Angeles, CA 90037. (213) 752-5811.
Instituted in 1972, the ASFFHF is composed of twelve state groups and 3,000 members--actors, writers, producers, directors, special effects personnel, and others connected with the film industry, as well as educators and researchers. The academy is primarily concerned with recognizing outstanding work in the science fiction, fantasy, and horror film genres relating to the fields of acting, music, direction, writing, cinematography, special effects, makeup, film criticism, set decoration and design, stop motion animation, publicity, and advertising. This goal is accomplished in part through the presentation of the Saturn Awards, the Golden Scroll Awards, and the Science Fiction Film Awards. It also conducts lectures and seminars, maintains a hall of fame, and publishes a quarterly newsletter.

American Film Institute. Jean Firstenberg, Director. John F. Kennedy for the Performing Arts, Washington, D.C. 20566. (213) 856-7706. Toll Free: (800) 774-4234. Fax: (202) 659-1970.

A private corporation, established in 1967 and comprising more than 135,000 members, dedicated to preserving and nurturing the country's artistic resources in film and video. Its activities include sponsoring an intensive two-year course in filmmaking and film theory; promoting the study of cinema as an art form with its own aesthetics, history, and techniques by offering resources and seminars to educators; brings notable films to public attention through The American Film Institute Theatre in the Kennedy Center; produces touring film series; conducts television and video services to develop new audiences for the video arts; spotlights innovations; cooperates with other agencies concerned with television and video arts; and maintains the Center for Advanced Film and Television Studies. Also offers prestigious awards (AFI Maya Deren Award, Life Achievement Award, Robert M. Bennett Award) and publishes the following works: *The AFI Catalog of Feature Films*, *Catalog of Motion Pictures Produced in the United States*, and *Getting Started in Film*.

Anthology Film Archives. Jonas Mekas, Director. 32 2nd Ave., New York, Y 10003. (212) 505-5181. Fax: (212) 477-2714.
The museum, founded in 1970, is funded by foundations such as the National Endowment for the Arts and the New York State Council on the Arts. In addition to providing resources to scholars and the public at large, it facilitates the preservation of new cutting edge works, operates two theatres that run new material and films from the AFA collection, and conducts research programs. Publications include the *Legend of Maya Deren, Vol. I.*

Association of Independent Video and Filmmakers. Ruby Lerner, Executive Director. 304 Hudson St., 6th Fl., New York, NY 10013. (212) 807-1400. Fax: (212) 463-8519. E-mail: aivffivf@aol.com. Website: http://www.aivf.org.
Founded in 1974, members include independent film- and videomakers, producers, directors, writers, and individuals involved in film and television. AIVF sponsors independent work, through financing and exhibitions, as a vital expression of American culture; works to increase, via the Foundation for Independent Video and Film, public appreciation of independent efforts; offers a Festival Bureau, seminars, and referrals; and maintains a resource center. Publishes the *Guide to Film and Video Distributors*, *Guide to International Film and Video Festivals*, *Guide to Video & Film Resources in Latin America and The Caribbean*, and *The Independent Film & Video Monthly* (10/year).

Association of Movie Imaging Archivists. c/o Gregory Lukow, Secretary. National Center for Film and Video Preservation, American Film Institute, 201 N. Western Ave., Box 27999, Los Angeles, CA 90027. (213) 856-7637. Fax: (213) 856-7616. Website: http://www.sc.library.unh.edu/amia/amia.htm.
The organization, established in 1991, seeks to preserve films while improving public awareness of archival imperatives through educational programs. Maintains a reference library and publishes the *AMIA Newsletter* (quarterly).

Black Filmmaker Foundation. Vallery Moore, Director. Tribeca Film Center, 670 Broadway, Ste. 304, New York, NY 10012. Fax: (212) 941-3943.

The foundation, established in 1978, nurtures the growth of an audience for works by black filmmakers through public screenings and the sponsorship of local and national film festivals. Also conducts educational programs, operates a Talent Directory to facilitate job referrals, and maintains a reference library. Publishes a monthly newsletter, *BFF News*.

Count Dracula Society. c/o Dr. Donald A. Reed, President. 334 W. 54th St., Los Angeles, CA 90037. (213) 752-5811.
Named for the central character in the nineteenth century Bra, Stoker novel, the society's approximately 1,000 members include academicians, teachers, writers, librarians, movie producers, and others devoted to the serious study of horror films and gothic literature. It presents the Ann Radcliff Awards in literature, movies, and television; the International Cinema Achievement Award; the Horace Walpole Gold Medal; and the Rev. Dr. Montague Summers Memorial Award. Affiliated with the Academy of Science Fiction, Fantasy, and Horror Films, the CDS maintains the Horror Hall of Fame and publishes *The Count Dracula Quarterly*. It was founded in 1962.

Film Arts Foundation. Gail Silva, Director. 346 9th St., 2nd Fl., San Francisco, CA 94103. (415) 552-8760. Fax: (415) 552-0882. E-mail: faf@igc.apc.org.
Founded in 1976, the FAF membership consists of 3,000-odd independent film- and videomakers. Activities include the provision of technical, educational, and information services; making available equipment for film and video production, editing, and screnning; and maintaining a reference library. Publishes the monthly periodical, *Release Print*.

Hollywood Studio Collectors Club. c/o Ralph E. Benner, Executive Officer. 3960 Laurel Canyon Blvd., Ste. 450, Studio City, CA 91614. (818) 990-5450.
The HSCC promotes interest in collecting movie memorabilia and related artifacts; conducts research on motion picture history; encourages trading, buying, and selling among members; exchanges relevant information with its 9,000-odd constituency and with film museums and halls of fame. Es tablished in 1957, it oversees a biographical archive on the cinema and publishes *Hollywood Studio Magazine*.

National Board of Review of Motion Pictures. c/o Inez Salinger Glucksman, President. P.O. Box 925, New York, NY 10024-0546. (212) 628-1594.
The board, formed in 1909, has approximately 8,500 members, including both general film enthusiasts and specialists interested in the technical and artistic aspects of the film industry. Publishes the journal, *Films in Review* (6/year).
Society for Cinema Studies. c/o Marcia Landy, Treasurer. University of Pittsburgh, 526 Cathedral of Learning, English Department, Pittsburgh, PA 15626.
Founded in 1959, the society is open to college faculty, film scholars, critics, archivists, and others interested in the history and criticism of the moving image. Its activities include facilitating the exchange of ideas and information, encouraging serious writing about film, and assisting students in film research and criticism. Publishes the quarterly journal, *Cinema Journal*.

Sundance Institute. c/o Gary Beer, Executive Vice President. P.O. Box 16450, Salt Lake City, UT 84116. (801) 328-3456. Fax: (801) 575-5175.

Through its sponsorship of programs in film, theatre, dance, and music, the institute supports the production of a diversified array of artistic, low-budget films and provides a disciplined and professional environment for participants, including the chance to collaborate with experienced practitioners. Publishes a semiannual newsletter.

ASSOCIATIONS AND SOCIETIES--TELEVISION

General

Academy of Television Arts and Sciences. c/o James L. Loper, Executive Director. 5220 Lankershim Blvd., North Hollywood, CA 91601. (818) 754-2800. Fax: (818) 761-2827. Website: http://www.emmys.org.

Established in 1948, ATAS is composed of more than 6,500 professionals in the television and film industry. Its service goals include advancing the arts and sciences of television through the delivery of education to the industry, the preservation of programming, the enhancement of community relations, and the nurturing of creative leadership in the industry. The academy presents the Primetime Emmy Awards, the Los Angeles Area Emmy Awards, and Student Video Awards, all on an annual basis. It sponsors the Television Academy Hall of Fame and maintains the Television Academy Archives and a collection of over 35,000 programs at UCLA. Internships are offered to students educational offerings include symposia, luncheon speakers series, faculty seminars, workshops, and meetings devoted to resolving the problems of various crafts. Publications include *Debut*, a semiannual newsletter focusing on the educational programs of the Academy; *Emmy Directory* (annual); and *Emmy Magazine* (bimonthly), a general interest magazine of the TV industry.

Associated Press Broadcasters. c/o Jim Williams, Vice President & Director. 1825 K St., NW, Ste. 710, Washington, D.C. 20006-1253. (202) 736-1100; (800) 821-4747. Fax: (202) 736-1107.

Founded in 1941, APB includes over 6,000 members and 50 state groups. Operates as a liaison between radio and television stations with AP membership and representatives of those stations in order to facilitate the delivery of accurate and impartial news.

Association of America's Public Television Stations. David Brugger, President. 1350 Connecticut Ave., NW, Ste. 200, Washington, D.C. 2036. (202) 887-1700. Fax: (202) 293-2422. E-mail: info@apts.org. Website: http://www.universe.digex.net.

Active since 1980, AAPTS is comprised of public television licensees concerned with an organized approach to planning and research, and preparing and disseminating information to government, the press, and the public. Updates information on the public television system with respect to licensee characteristics, financing, and industry trends, and makes projections on system growth and income. Publishes the quarterly newsletters *Communique* and *Transitions*; and monthly newsletter, *Update*; and the annual booklet, *Research Studies*.

Broadcast Pioneers. Gordon H. Hastings, President and CEO. 296 Old Church Rd., Greenwich, CT 10019. (203) 862-8577. Fax: (203) 629-5739.
Formed in 1942, membership is open to professionals serving at least fifteen years in broadcasting. Established the Broadcasting Industry Reference Center. Sponsors the Annual Golden Mike Award and the Broadcasters' Foundation which assists broadcast veterans needing aid. Published the quarterly newsletter, *On the Air*.

Cable and Telecommunications: A Marketing Society. Char Beales, President.
201 N. Union, Ste. 440, Alexandria, VA 22314. (703) 549-4200. Fax: (703) 684-1167.
The membership, 4,200 in all, consists of marketing and operations professionals within the cable television industry. Founded in 1975, it facilitates communication of marketing and operations ideas among members and conducts regional, general management, and research seminars. Publishes *CTAM Pulse* and *CTAM Quarterly Journal*.

Hollywood Radio and Television Society. c/o Oliver Crawford, Executive Director.
5315 Laurel Canyon Blvd., Ste. 202, North Hollywood, CA 91607. (818) 769-4313.
Founded in 1947, this group of approximately 1,000 members includes those involved in radio, television, broadcasting, competitions, and monthly luncheons featuring top industry and government speakers. It bestows annual International Broadcasting Awards for the best radio and television commercials. Publications include the quarterly *Spike*, and two annuals, the *Hollywood Radio and Television Society Roster* and *International Broadcasting Awards Book*.

National Academy of Television Arts and Sciences. John Cannon, President. 111
W. 57th St., Ste. 1020, New York, NY 10019. (212) 586-8424. (212) 246-8129.
NATAS, instituted in 1947, consists of persons engaged in television performing, art directing, cinematography, directing, taping, tape editing, choreography, engineering, film editing, music, production, and writing. It fosters artistic, cultural, educational, and technological progress within the medium; sponsors the Emmy Awards, maintains a research library, and organizes workshops and seminars. Publishes a bimonthly newsletter and *NATAS News* (quarterly).

National Association of Broadcasters. Edward O. Fritts, CEO & President. 1771 N. St., NW, Washington, D.C. 20036. (202) 429-5300. Fax: (202) 429-5343.
Established in 1922, the organization is open to representatives of radio and television stations and networks; among the associate members are equipment and program producers. Activities include serving as an information resource to the industry, monitoring and reporting on broadcasting developments, maintaining the Broadcasting Hall of Fame, and administering a minority placement service and employment clearinghouse. Publishes the *Member Services Catalog* (annual), *Broadcast Engineering Conference Proceedings* (annual), and the weekly journal, *TV Today*.

National Broadcast Association for Community Affairs. Cocoa, Florida.
Comprised of professionals from radio and television industries concerned with promoting public affairs programming and improving community relations. Sponsors

educational programs and an annual Community Service Award. A quarterly newsletter, *NBACA News*, disseminates information on industry issues, profiles of notable public affairs projects, and how-to features.

National Cable Television Association. S. Decker Anstrom, President and CEO. 1724 Massachusetts Ave., NW, Washington, D.C. 20036. (202) 775-3550. Fax: (202) 775-3695.
The organization, formed in 1952, includes cable operators, programmers, and cable networks. Cable hardware suppliers and distributors are associate members; brokerage and law firms and financial institutions are affiliate members; cooperative arrangements exists with state and regional cable television associations. NCTA facilitates the exchange of experiences and opinions through research, study, discussion and publications; represents the cable industry before Congress, the Federal Communications Commission, and various courts; conducts a research program along with the National Academy of Cable Programming; works to deter cable signal theft and develop antipiracy materials; and disseminates promotional aids and information on legal, legislative, and regulatory matters. Publishes the newsletter, *TechLine* (10/year), and monographs such as *Careers in Cable* and *FCC Cable Rules*.

National Cable Television Institute. Don Oden, Dan. 801 W. Mineral Ave., Littleton, CO 80120-4501. (303) 797-9393. Fax: (303) 797-9394. Website: http://www.ncti.com.
Makes available career training resources and courses in fields ranging from customer service procedures to optical fiber system design, installation, and maintenance. Publishes the book, *Spanish/English CATV Dictionary.*

NATPE International. Bruce Johansen, Contact. 2425 Olympic Blvd., Ste. 550E, Santa Monica, CA 90404. (310) 453-4440. Fax: (310) 453-5258. Website: http://www.natpe.org.
Founded in 1963, the organization is open to program directors of TV stations, networks, and multiple station groups; those engaged in television programming or production for companies holding voting membership; and representatives of related businesses (e.g., station personnel, advertising agencies, film and package show producers and distributors, research groups). Focuses on improving television programming through the discussion of ideas and exchange of information regarding programming, production, and related fields; maintains the NATPE Educational Foundation; and sponsors internships, a faculty development program, seminars, and an international exchange program. Publishes the *NATPE Pocket Guide Reps Groups Distributors* (semiannual), *NATPE Pocket Station Listing Guide* (quarterly), and the newsletter, *NATPE Monthly*.

Individual Programs

--*The Andy Griffith Show*

The Andy Griffith Show Rerun Watchers Club. c/o Jim Clark. 9 Music Sq., Ste. 146, Nashville, TN 37203-3203.

The club, founded in 1979, is centered on watching and promoting the broadcast of reruns of the show, which originally ran from 1960 to 1968. TAGSRWC also facilitates communication regarding the program among its 20,000-odd members, sponsors polls and lectures, maintains an archive, and publishes a newsletter, *The Bullet* (3/year).

--Dark Shadows

Dark Shadows Fan Club. c/o Louis Wendruck, President. P.O. Box 69A04, Dept. EA, West Hollywood, CA 90069. (213) 650-5112. E-mail: GayBoylaca@aol.com. Since its inception in 1987, the organization has provided a forum for fans of the gothic television serial which aired on ABC from 1966-1971. It holds meetings which enable the 20,000 members to meet the show's actors; disseminates memorabilia; maintains a reference library, computerized mailing list, and a website (http://members.aol.com/GayBoyLACA/index2.html); and publishes the quarterly newsletter, *The Dark Shadow Announcement*.

Dark Shadows Official Fan Club. c/o Ann Wilson, Executive Director. P.O. Box 92, Maplewood, NJ 07040. (201) 762-7208.
The club, established in 1982, focuses on preserving the memory of the original program, the 1990s revival series, and feature film interpretations. Activities include the provision of news updates to the 30,000-odd members, the donation of convention proceeds to various charities, maintenance of a memorabilia archive and reference library, and publication of two periodicals, *Shadowgram* and *World of Dark Shadows*.

--The Prisoner

Six of One Club: The Prisoner Appreciation Society. c/o Bruce A. Clark, Coordinator. 871 Clover Dr., North Wales, PA 19454-2749. (215) 699-2527. Fax: (215) 699-2272. E-mail: sixofone@netreach.net. Website: http://www.netreach.net/~sixofone. Founded in 1977, the club is dedicated to analysis of the series' seventeen episodes. Sponsors an annual conference and produces compact discs (soundtrack music) and interviews on video. Publications include the quarterly magazine, *In the Village*, and books such as *The Making of the Prisoner* and *The Prisoner Episode Guide*.

--Star Trek

Star Trek: The Official Fan Club. c/o Daniel H. Madsen, President. P.O. Box 111000, Aurora, CO 80042. (303) 341-1813.
The club, formed in 1980, is composed of more than 50,000 fans of *Star Trek* (which originally aired on NBC from 1966 to 1969) and *Star Trek: The Next Generation*. Its primary role is to keep members informed about the program, cast members, and film spin-offs. Activities include the operation of pen pal and actor forwarding services, the maintenance of a library and biographical archives, sponsorship of competitions, and the compilation of statistics. It publishes *The Official Star Trek Magazine* (bimonthly, also available online) and *The Star Trek Fan Club Merchandise Catalog* (bimonthly).

Star Trek WelCommittee. c/o Shirley S. Maiewski, Chairperson. P.O. Drawer 12, Saranac, MI 48881. (413) 247-5339.

The STW functions as a cent ral information center whose sixty- five-odd volunteer workers answer fans' questions about *Star Trek*. Founded in 1972, its departments include College and Library Programming, Convention Listing, Costume, Editors and Contributors Exchange, Foreign, Library Computer/General, Library Computer/Science and Technology, Military Fan Liaison, Newsclipping Service, Penpal Listing Service, Personal Computer, Sight Loss Services, Star Trek Educational Programs, Zine Acquisition, and Zine Publishing Information. Sponsors a quarterly mail auction of Star Trek merchandise and memorabilia and publishes the following: *Directory of Star Trek Organizations* (semiannual), *The Fan's Little Golden Guide to Throwing Your Own Con*, *How to Start a Club*, *History of the STW*, *The Neofan's Guide to Star Trek Fandom*, *Protocols: A Guide to Fanzines*, and *So You Want Publicity*.

Starfleet. c/o Michael D. Smith, President. 200 Hiawatha Blvd., Oakland, NJ 07436-3643. (201) 337-3645. Fax: (201) 337-0760. E-mail: cs@sfi.org. Website: http://www.sfi.org.

Composed of 16 regional groups, 225 local groups, and 7,000 members, it is open to anyone interested in science fiction films and television programs, particularly the television and motion picture series *Star Trek*. The organization conducts service activities, bestows awards, and produces the bimonthly *Starfleet Communique*. It was established in 1974.

Starfleet Command. c/o Rita Cawthon-Clark, Chief of Staff. P.O. Box 180637, Casselberry, FL 32718-0637. (407) 677-4169.

For space and science fiction enthusiasts, the SFC upholds the Star Trek philosophy of "Infinite Diversity through Infinite Combinations" and its application to everyday living. Formed in 1974, the 2,500 members, twelve regional groups, one state group, and 100 local groups attempt to help individuals realize their full potential; promote the peaceful exploration and use of space; support the development of a permanent working space station or moon base; and encourage the support of environmental, conservation, and resource management programs. Programs include charitable activities, bestowing awards, maintaining a library, serving as a forum for the exchange of ideas and information, and sponsoring an annual convention. The SFC publishes *Starfleet Communications* (quarterly) and a newsletter covering organization news and activities, science and space-related issues, and Star Trek updates.

ATLASES--TELEVISION

Warren Publishing's Cable and Station Coverage Atlas, 1995. Warren Publishing, 1995. il. $399.00. ISBN 0911486909.

Provides concise data regarding UHF/VHF and cable television stations in the United States.

BIBLIOGRAPHIES/FILMOGRAPHIES/VIDEOGRAPHIES--
FILM INDUSTRY

Altomara, Rita Ecke. Hollywood on the Palisades: A
Filmography of Silent Features Made in Fort Lee, New
Jersey, 1903-1927. New York: Garland, 1983. 226p. il., name
and title indexes. (Garland Reference Library of the Humanities,
Vol. 368) ISBN 0-8240-9225-2.
The work includes a brief introduction, which surveys the
origins of filmmaking in the town, and three primary listings:
"Stellar Attractions" (films starring established actors), "Early
Auteurs" (notable directors working there early in their careers),
and "Supporting Features" (more obscure productions).
Although credits are sometimes sketchy, many unique titles
cited here are not recorded in other sources.

Ellis, Jack C., Charles Derry, and Sharon Kern. The Film
Book Bibliography 1940-1975. Metuchen, NJ: Scarecrow
Press, 1979. 764p. $28.50. ISBN 0-8108-1127-8.
A useful guide which cites and classifies books, monographs
and dissertations in English on movies from 1940 to 1975. Nearly
5,500 citations are given, making this a good reference source
for reseachers delving into movie literature. The categories
covered are Reference, Film Technique and Technology, Film
Industry, Film History, Film Classifications; Biography,
Analysis and Interview; Individual Films, Film Theory and
Criticism, Film and Society, and Film and Education. It is too
bad this work has not been updated.

Friedweald, Will, and Jerry Beck. The Warner Brothers
Cartoons. Metuchen, NJ: Scarecrow Press, 1981. 287p.
$15.00. ISBN 0-8108-1396-3.
A superb filmography listing all of the over 850 films in
Warner Bros.' "Looney Tunes" and "Merry Melodies" cartoon
series. For each title release date, credits and plot synopsis
is supplied. Running from 1929 to 1969, the book includes
such cartoon characters as Bugs Bunny, Porky Pig, Tweety,
Daffy Duck, The Roadrunner, and Bosko. This volume will
delight cartoon buffs.

Pierce, David, ed. The Film Daily Yearbook Guide to
the Thirties. Laurel, MD: David Pierce, 1986. 150p. $25.00.
This extremely useful research guide takes the release
information for films included in each of the 1930s *Film Daily*
yearbooks and combines them into a single volume. For each
year all the movies covered in the yearbooks are listed alphabetically

with credits for each film. For each year is also a
list of all the films released by individual companies, including
imports. A similar volume was also done for the 1940s.

Rainey, Buck. The Shoot-Em-Ups Ride Again. Metuchen, NJ:
Scarecrow Press, 1990. 319p. $62.50. ISBN 0-8108-2132-X.
A sequel to the author's earlier *Shoot-Em-Ups* (q.v.), this
work supplements that major effort to record movie credits for
the Western film. The author not only adds movies released
after the first volume but includes additions and corrections
to the base work and magnifies the list of Continental Westerns
in the 1978 book. Western television series and telefilms are
also chronicled. A worthy companion to the first book. This
volume was also issued in a softbound edition by The World
of Yesterday ($19.95pa.; ISBN 0-936505-12-5).

Scheuer, Steven H. The Complete Guide To Videocassette
Movies. New York: Henry Holt, 1987. 671p. $19.95 pap.
ISBN 0-8050-0110-7.
Listing more than 5,000 feature films available on video
cassette, this volume provides casts and a summary for each
title plus a rating. While this volume may have had some value
at the time of its publication, it is long out-of-date since
so many more titles are now on the video shelves.

Scheuer, Steven H. Movie Blockbusters. New York:
Bantam, 1983. 127p. $5.95 pap.
The top 50 best money making movies up to the time of
this thin paperback's publication are included. Each film
is briefly discussed, including cast, credits, and any awards
or nominations. Ironically, no financial data is provided.

Welch, Jeffrey Egan. Literature and Film: An Annotated
Bibliography, 1909-1977. New York: Garland, 1981. 315p.
Index. (Garland Reference Library of the Humanities, Vol. 241)
ISBN 0-8240-9478-6.
The listing covers notable monographs and articles published
in North America and Great Britain between 1909 and 1977 that
are concerned with the relationship between films and works of
literature. The 1,102 entries (not counting 133 dissertations
produced from 1939 onwards, which appear in a separate listing)
are arranged chronologically by year and subdivided by author's
name. An alphabetical list of fiction writers. and the films derived
from their works, functions as a subject index and provides titles of
both the works and the films; the names of the director, scenarist,
and producer; and the film's year of release.

Wescott, Steven D. A Comprehensive Bibliography of
Music for Film and Television. Detroit, MI: Information
Coordinators, 1985. 432p. index. (Detroit Studies in Music
Bibliography, No. 5) ISBN 0-89990-027-5.
The work is concerned with music's role as a dramatic
element in film and television. The 6,340 citations have been
organized into three main categories: "History" (dealing with
surveys and critiques), "Composer," and "Themes" (aesthetics,
special topics, and research).

Checklists

Baer, D. Richard. The Film Buff's Checklist of Motion
Pictures (1912-1979). Hollywood, CA: Hollywood
Film Archive, 1972. 322p. ISBN 0-913616-03-6.
Originally published in 1972 as *The Film Buff's Bible*,
this volume is nothing more than an illustrated list of film titles.
Entries included title, release year and company, whether
black and white or color, running time, origin, stars, alternate
titles, and a rating system. Its effectiveness is compromised by
the absence of any updated edition.

Martin, Len D. The Allied Artists Checklist. Jefferson,
NC: McFarland & Co., 1993. 232p. $45.00. ISBN
0-89950-782-4.
Useful compilation of all the feature films and short
subjects released by Allied Artists between 1947 and 1978.
Cast and credits, plot and comments are provided for each
Title. Appendices include titles by release date, movie
series, western stars' series, Academy Award winners and
nominees. Thoroughly indexed, the volume is laced with
interesting illustrations.

Martin, Len D. The Columbia Checklist. Jefferson, NC:
McFarland & Co., 1991. 647p. $82.00. ISBN
0-89550-556-2.
Impressive filmography of all the feature films, serials,
cartoons and short subjects from Columbia Pictures Corporation
between 1922 and 1988. Information listed for each title
includes cast, credits, plot, notes, and release dates. For
cartoons the release date, director, producer and series is
provided. Also included are lists of Columbia series, western
stars and their series films, comedy stars and their series
titles, and awards. With a thorough index, this is a major
work representing one of Hollywood's most prolific studios.

Martin, Len D. The Republic Pictures Checklist: Features, Serials, Cartoons, Short Subjects and Training Films of Republic Pictures Corporation, 1935-1959. Jefferson, NC: McFarland, 1997. 383p. il. $65.00. ISBN 0-7864-0438-8.
Continuing his series of volumes giving filmographies of Hollywood studios, Martin has compiled a thorough checklist of the 946 feature films of Republic Pictures plus its serials (66), cartoons (5), short subjects 51), and training films (16). In addition, the work supplies several useful appendices, including a chronological list of release dates, western stars, and their series titles, Academy Award nominations and winners and a list of the studio's various series films. For features and serials information for each title includes release date, whether black and white or color, director, associate producer, script writer(s), cast, brief plot synopsis, alternate titles and, in some cases, notations. Serials also include chapter titles. Thoroughly indexed, the volume is a well written, concise and valuable Republic Pictures filmography. Attractively illustrated with posters and lobby card reproductions.

Okuda, Ted. The Monogram Checklist: The Films of Monogram Pictures Corporation, 1931-1952. Jefferson, NC: McFarland, 1987. 399p. $55.00. ISBN 0-89950-286-5.
Following a brief historical overview of the studio, all of The movies released by Monogram Pictures are chronicled in the order of issuance, including cast, credits, and plot. A title index lists all films in alphabetical order with release year and entry number. Thorough coverage of a popular low budget film studio which became Allied Artists.

Sigoloff, Marc. The Films of the Seventies: A Filmography of American and Canadian Films 1970-1979. Jefferson, NC: McFarland, 1984. 432p. index. $29.95. ISBN 0-89950-095-1.
The almost 1,000 alphabetically arranged entries include cast lists, credits, plot synopses, and information regarding box office performance and critical reception. Films considered by Sigoloff to be "out of the mainstream" (and, therefore, irrelevant to his attempt to provide an overview of the decade through its films) have been omitted; e.g., exploitation films, sex-oriented movies, low-budget independent films, animation features, documentaries.

BIBLIOGRAPHIES--TELEVISION

General

Cooper, Thomas W., with others. Television & Ethics: A Bibliography. Boston: G.K. Hall, 1988. 203p. program and subject-author indexes. ISBN 0-8161-8966-8. Rather than focusing on how ethics influence plotting and character development in programming, the tool is primarily concerned with the impact of television upon the viewer along with the ethical implications of such power. The main bibliographic section, including 1,170 articles (nearly 500 of which are annotated, largely to clarify the content of the more ambiguous titles), is subdivided into the following headings: Ethic Contexts--classical ethics; professional ethics; communication and mass media ethics including codes; journalism ethics; teaching ethics--and Television and Ethics--practices and programming; advertising; children and television; television entertainment; television news; television politics and government; ethics and television's effects; regulations, law, and courtroom coverage; public and educational television; and documents. Covering the period from classical Greece to 1987, the compilation includes the significant research, dialogues, and case studies within the industry.

Hill, George H., and Sylvia Saverson Hill. Blacks on Television: a Selectively Annotated Bibliography. Metuchen, NJ: Scarecrow, 1985. 223p. program, author, personal name, and organization indexes.
Inventories 156 books, dissertations and theses, scholarly articles, and approximately 2,700 citations to articles in the African American and general press. The newspaper and magazine section is arranged by topics (e.g., news, sports). Appendixes include a listing of Emmy winners by category as well as television and cable stations owned by African Americans.

Hill, George H., Lorraine Raglin, and Chas Floyd Johnson. Black Women in Television: An Illustrated History and Bibliography. New York: Garland, 1990. 168p. Utilizes the general format of *Blacks on Television* in focusing on African-American women's contributions to the medium.

Kittross, John M. A Bibliography of Theses & Dissertations in Broadcasting, 1920-1973. Washington, D.C.: Broadcast Education Association, 1978. [238]p. keyword- in-title, year of completion, and broad topics indexes.
Inventories approximately 4,300 Ph.D dissertations and master's theses earned at American universities from 1920-1973 which primarily concerned with some aspect of broadcasting. The entries, a substantial number of which specifically cover the television medium, are arranged alphabetically by author.

Peer, Kurt. TV Tie-Ins: A Bibliography of American TV Tie-in Paperbacks. Neptune, 1997. 384p. $24.95. indexes. ISBN 0965453634.
The work inventories some 1,400 mass- market paperbacks based on or issued in conjunction with a TV series. Arrangement by series, most of paperbacks are either

original novels featuring series characters or novelizations of specific episodes. A wide range of genres are represented, including humor, cookbooks, and star biographies. The text is enhanced by an introduction tracing the development of television and paperback book industry. Although book values have not been incorporated, *TV Tie-Ins* is more focused than its chief competitor, Randall Larson's *Films into Books: An Analytical Bibliography of Film Novelizaions, Movie and TV Tie-Ins* (1995).

Shiers, George, and May Shiers, comps. Early Television: A Bibliographic Guide to 1940. New York: Garland, 1997. 616p. name and subject indexes. (Garland Reference Library of Social Science, v. 582) $95.00. ISBN 0-8240-7782-2.
Despite the death of George Shiers prior to completion of this project, it serves as the definitive compilation of resource materials (8,633 citatio ns overall) concerned with the medium from 1817--the date of the discovery of light-sensitive selenium--to 1995. In addition to English language entries, the French, German, and Italian literature have been included. The work is comprised of chronologically arranged chapters (with annual breakdowns between 1927-1939); the final chapter (20), entitled "Distant View, 1940-1995," provides superficial coverage with only 250 references. Each chapter includes an introductory essay (except 1932-1939) focusing on notable developments, patent applications, and publishing trends in addition to a chronology of events (except 1936-1939). The work is further enhanced with introductions by Tony Bridgewater, onetime chief engineer for the British Broadcasting Corporation, and George Shiers ("Understanding a Century of Television").

Signorielli, Nancy, comp. and ed. Role Portrayal and Stereotyping on Television: An Annotated Bibliography of Studies Relating to Women, Minorities, Aging, Sexual Behavior, Health, and Handicaps. Westport, CT: Greenwood, 1985. 214p. author and subject indexes. (Bibliographies and Indexes in Sociology, No. 5) ISBN 0-313-24855-9.
The volume's 423 entries are organized into five parts: "Women and Sex-Roles," "Racial and Ethnic Minorities," "Aging and Age-Roles," "Sexual Behavior and Orientation," and "Health an Handicaps" (each arranged alphabetically by author). The entries, consisting largely of research published in journals, books, and federal documents, describe sampling techniques and findings (where relevant).

Sparks, Kenneth R. A Bibliography of Doctoral Dissertations in Television and Radio. 3rd ed. Syracuse, NY: School of Journalism, Syracuse University [1971] 119p. author index.
A classified arrangement of approximately 900 doctoral theses produced up through June 1970 which cover television and/or the radio.

Videographies

Video Yesteryear [catalog]. Sandy Hook, CT: Video Yesteryear. Annual with irregular supplements. 250+p./issue. Available free upon request (800-243-0987).
The source lists more than 1,200 vintage titles available on the VHS videotape format. The program material includes classic films from the silent and pre-World War II eras,

cult films, television shows, compilations of animation and other special interest subjects, and so on. The annotations appended to each entry possess considerable reference value; the majority of titles also include black-and-white stills.

BIOGRAPHICAL SOURCES--FILM INDUSTRY

Agan, Patrick. The Decline and Fall of the Love Goddesses. Los Angeles: Pinnacle Books, 1979. 286p. Biographies of ten beautiful actresses whose lives and careers eventually turned to tragedy, make up this illustrated volume. Covers Rita Hayworth, Jayne Mansfield, Betty Hutton, Linda Darnell, Veronica Lake, Betty Grable, Susan Hayward, Dorothy Dandridge, Frances Farmer, and Marilyn Monroe. Filmographies for each star are also provided.

Belton, John. Cinema Stylists. Metuchen, NJ: Scarecrow Press, 1983. 394p. $35.00. ISBN 0-8108-1585-0. Interesting collection of essays on the work of various directors and performers with emphasis on their visual styles. Among those studied are Alfred Hitchcock, Samuel Fuller, Douglas Sirk, Edgar G. Ulmer, D.W. Griffith, Frank Borgaze, Joseph H. Lewis, Otto Preminger, Don Siegel, Howard Hawks, Jean Renoir, and Charles Chaplin. An especially interesting essay examines the screen persona of John Wayne.

Belton, John. The Hollywood Professionals, Volume 3. London, England: Tantivy Press, 1974. 182p. $2.95 pap. ISBN 0-498-01448-7. Another well done entry in Tantivy Press' "The Hollywood Professionals" series, this one studies the careers of directors Howard Hawks, Frank Borgaze, and Edgar G. Ulmer. Chapters on each of the directors cover their work as well as individual titles and thorough filmographies are provided for each.

Cameron-Wilson, James. Young Hollywood. Lanham, MD: Madison Books, 1994. 224p. il. $34.95. ISBN 1-56833-038-3. One hundred contemporary Hollywood stars are profiled in this volume, which includes biographies and filmographies (television and video) along with numerous photographs. The author's essays are concise and informative and among those included are Patricia Arquette, Kevin Bacon, Alec Baldwin, Drew Barrymore, Matthew Broderick, Phoebe Cates, Tom Cruise, Jamie Lee Curtis, Geena Davis, Bridget, Fonda, Jodie Foster, Darryl Hannah, Timothy Hutton, Val Kilmer, Jennifer Jason Leigh, Rob Lowe, Madonna, Demi Moore, Eddie Murphy, Sean Penn, Brad Pitt,

Julia Roberts, Winona Ryder, Sharon Stone, Patrick Swayze, Uma Thurman, and Jean-Claude Van Damme.

Canham, Kingsley. The Hollywood Professionals, Volume 1. London: Tantivy Press, 1973. 200p. $2.95 pap. ISBN 498-01204-2. Career profiles and filmographies for directors Michael Curtiz, Raoul Walsh and Henry Hathaway are provided in this well done work. The work of each of the three directors is anaylzed, all of them known for slick, high quality entertainment films. Recommended reading for those interested in any of the three directors.

Cary, Diana Serra. Hollywood's Children. Boston: Houghton Mifflin, 1979. 290p. $11.95. ISBN 0-395-27095-2. Former child star Baby Peggy relates the stories of other youngsters who became national idols as movie stars and the often sad and tragic results. Among those profiled are Jackie Coogan, Shirley Temple, Mickey Rooney, Judy Garland, Deanna Durbin, Jackie Cooper, Anne Shirley, and Edith Fellows. Among the saddest aspects of the volume is the continuing story of parents willing to sell their children to the movies in return for financial security.

Corneau, Ernest N. The Hall of Fame of Western Film Stars . North Quincy: MA: Christopher Publishing House, 1969. 307p. il. $9.75. ISBN 8158-0124-6. Fan- like attempt to cover the careers of dozens of cowboy films stars from the silent era into the late 1960s. The volume's is noteworthy in that it profiles so many performers but most of the writeups are rehashes from other publications. Dotted with photos, the book is only of peripheral interest to western film fans.

Crivello, Kirk. Fallen Angels. New York: Berkeley Books, 1990. 254p. $4.50 pap. ISBN 0-425-11968-8. Originally published in a hardcover edition in 1988, this well-written book studies the careers of fourteen Hollywood sex symbols who met with tragic ends. Those profiled include Marilyn Monroe, Jayne Mansfield, Barbara Payton, Gail Russell, Marie McDonald, Gia Scala, Inger Stevens, and Carole Landis. Thumbnail sketches are also provided for a number of other actresses under the title "Shattered Dreams."

Dixon, Wheeler W. The "B" Directors: A Biographical Dictionary. Metuchen, NJ: Scarecrow Press, 1985. 613p. $47.50. ISBN 0-8108-1835-3.

Fairly useful volume which gives brief summaries of the
careers of some 400 Hollywood directors who specialized in
making low budget cinema. A filmography is provided for each
with supposedly better titles highlighted. An appendix lists
major films cited in the text with release company, year, and
director.

Eells, George. Ginger, Loretta and Irene Who? New York:
G.P. Putnam's Sons, 1976. 393p. $9.95. ISBN: 399-11822-5.
Five female stars (Ginger Rogers, Miriam Hopkins, Ruth
Etting, Loretta Young, and Irene Manning) are given in-depth
career studies in this informative and very readable volume.
A lengthy appendix includes filmographies, discographies,
stage appearances, etc., for the actresses. Well-done fan-type
volume although the author seems a bit harsh to Ginger Rogers.

Lahue, Kalton C. Riders of the Range: The Sagebrush
Heroes of the Sound Screen. Cranbury, NJ: A.S. Barnes, 1973.
259p. il. $10.00. ISBN 0-498-07931-7.
Illustrated with over 250 photos, this volume gives
cursory biographies of over two dozen cowboy film stars of
sound movies. Among those included are Bob Allen, Gene Autry,
Donald Barry, William Boyd, Johnny Mack Brown, Sunset Carson,
Buster Crabbe, William Elliott, Tom Keene, Allan Lane, Lash
Larue, George O'Brien, Tex Ritter, Roy Rogers, Randolph Scott,
Charles Starrett, and Whip Wilson.

Lahue, Kalton C. Winners of the West: The Sagebrush
Heroes of the Silent Screen. Cranbury, NJ: A.S. Barnes.,
1970. 353p. il. $10.00. ISBN 0-498-07396-3.
Fairly informative biographies of more than three dozen
silent film western heroes make up this book along with numerous
photos. Those profiled include Art Acord, Broncho Billy Anderson,
Harry Carey, Edmund Cobb, William Desmond, Franklyn
Farnum, Hoot Gibson, William S. Hart, Jack Hoxie, Buck Jones,
J. Warren Kerrigan, Ken Maynard, Tim McCoy, Tom Mix, Jack Perrin,
Buddy Roosevelt, Bob Steele, Tom Tyler, Wally Wales, and Jay
Wilsey (Buffalo Bill Jr.).

Langman, Larry. A Guide to American Film Directors: The
Sound Era: 1929-1979. Metuchen, NJ: Scarecrow Press, 1981.
2 volumes: 391p.; 327p. $29.50. ISBN 0-8108-1476-6.
More than 2,000 film directors in the sound era are included in
volume one of this work with filmographies that list their movies
and release years. Volume two alphabetically lists all the titles
included in volume one with release date and director's name.

Maltin, Leonard. The Great Movie Comedians. New
York: Crown, 1978. 238p. il. ISBN 0-517-532417.
Informative biographies of twenty-two of Hollywood's
legendary laugh makers are included in this book along with
filmographies and nearly 200 photographs. The subjects include
Charlie Chaplin, Mabel Normand, Fatty Arbuckle, Harold Lloyd,
Laurel & Hardy, Mae West, the Marx Brothers, W.C. Fields,
The Three Stooges, Abbott & Costello, Bob Hope, and Red
Skelton. Less remembered comedians like Charley Chase,
Raymond Griffith, and Joe E. Brown are also given their due.

Maltin, Leonard. Movie Comedy Teams. New York:
New American Library, 1985. 373p. $9.95 pap. ISBN
0-452-25694-1.
Revised and updated edition of the work originally published
in 1970 by Signet. With informative text, good photos and
thorough filmographies, the author provides the histories of
noted movie comedy duos like Laure and Hardy, Wheeler and
Woolsey, the Marx Brothers, Thelma Todd and partners Patsy Kelly
and ZaSu Pitts, the Three Stooges, the Ritz Brothers, and Abbott
and Costello. Lesser teams like Moran and Mack, Smith and Dale
and the Wiere Brothers are also included as is the dubious
insertion of Cheech and Chong.

Maltin, Leonard, ed. The Real Stars. New York: Curtis
Books, 1973. 320p. $1.50 pap.
A compilation of career articles and filmographies first
published in *Film Fan Monthly*. Among those profiled are
Sara Allgood, Edgar Buchanan, Joyce Compton, Billy Gilbert,
Rex Ingram, Una Merkel, Mabel Paige, Gale Sondergaard,
Grady Sutton, and Blanche Yurka.

Maltin, Leonard, ed. The Real Stars #2. New York: Curtis
Books, 1973. 287p. $1.50 pap.
Follow- up to the above book, this one reprints articles
Film Fan Monthly, *Screen Facts*, and *Filmograph* magazines.
The subjects profiled include Iris Adrian, Lionel Atwill, Roy
Barcroft, Sydney Greenstreet, Keye Luke, Maria Ouspenskaya,
and Max Terhune.

Maltin, Leonard, and Bann, Richard W. Our Gang: The Life
and Times Of The Little Rascals. New York: Crown, 1977.
288p. il. $12.95. ISBN 0-517-526751.
A history of Hal Roach's famous "Our Gang" series, which
ran from 1922 to 1944, is provided in this outstanding study.

Each of the Gang's 221 films are covered and biographical information is provided for many of the series regulars like Jackie Cooper, Chubby Chaney, Spanky McFarland, Alfalfa Switzer, and Darla Hood. The best book to date on this enduring series.

McCarthy, John, ed. The Fearmakers. New York: St. Martin's Press, 1994. 198p. il. $14.95 pap. ISBN 0-312-11272-6. Movie directors known for terror and suspense films are covered individually here in a series of essays which vary in quality; each contains a limited filmography. Among the directors discussed are Tod Browning, Roland West, James Whale, Roger Corman, Jack Arnold, William Castle, Terence Fisher, Roman Polanski, Dario Argento, and John Carpenter. The contributors include Ken Hanke, Raymond G. Cabana Jr., Michael J. Collins, and Bruce G. Hallenbeck. This oversized paperback contains a number of interesting b/w pictures.

McCarthy, John, ed. The Sleaze Merchants. New York: St. Martin' Press, 1995. 289p. $16.95 pap. ISBN 0-312-11893-7. Like the above work, this volume covers the individual careers of several film dir ectors. In this case, however, they are associated with exploitation filmmaking and range from old-timers like Sam Katzman (who was basically a producer) to cult figures such as Edward D. Wood Jr., Al Adamson, John Waters, and Jess Franco. There is also coverage of more recent helmsmen like Fred Olen Ray, Jim Wynorski, and David DeCoteau. The contributors include Ken Hanke, Walter L. Gay and Bruce G. Hallenbeck. As with the previous book there are lots of Pictures, but the text is a bit more fun due to the subject matter.

McClure, Arthur F., and Ken D. Jones. Heroes, Heavies and Sagebrush: A Pictorial History of the "B" Western Players. South Brunswick, NJ: A.S. Barnes, 1972. 351p. $15.00. ISBN 0-498-07787-X. This volume provides brief biographical sketches of actors associated with the western genre, with plenty of illustrations. There are biographical sections on heroes, sidekicks, heavies, Indians and assorted players. Filmographies are provided for each entry.

McDonald, Archie P., ed. Shooting Stars: Heroes and Heroines of Western Film. Bloomington, IN: Indiana University Press, 1987. 265p. ISBN 0-253-20415-1. The biographical and cinematic lives of several Western film stars are presented in this volume, including John Wayne,

Gene Autry, Clint Eastwood, Ken Maynard, Randolph Scott, Audie Murphy, and Burt Lancaster. Women in westerns, portrayed by actresses like Barbara Stanwyck and Jane Russell, are also covered as are television westerns. The chapters are well researched and informative.

Mercer, Jane. Great Lovers of the Movies. New York: Crescent, 1975. 176p. il. ISBN 0-517-131269.
This pictorial history, with some photos in color, profiles the screen careers of nearly two dozen male stars who were among the movies' greatest on-screen lovers. Among them are Douglas Fairbanks, Rudolph Valentino, Ramon Novarro, John Barrymore, John Gilbert, Ronald Colman, Clark Gable, Cary Grant, Errol Flynn, Robert Taylor, Tyrone Power, Robert Mitchum, Rock Hudson, and Clint Eastwood. Filmographies for each player are included.

Parish, James Robert, with Kingsley Canham, Lorenzo Codelli, Herve Dumont, Pierre Guinle, Norman Miller, Jeanne Passalacqua, and Florence Solomon. Film Directors Guide: Western Europe. Metuchen, NJ: Scarecrow Press, 1976. 292p. $20.00. ISBN 0-8108-0908-7.
In the same format as the previous volume, this book lists scores of directors from Western Europe with credits through the mid-1970s. While a good source for credits, some cult directors like Jess Franco and Jean Rollin are not included.

Parish, James Robert, with Kingsley Canham, Herve Dumont, Jeanne Passalacqua, Linda J. Sandahal, and Florence Solomon. Film Actors Guide: Western Europe. Metuchen, NJ: Scarecrow Press, 1977. 621p. il. $24.00. ISBN 0-8108-1044-1.
Nearly 600 film actors from Western Europe are included in this tome in alphabetical order. Listed is the person's real name, if different from their screen one, birth and death dates, and a chronological list of their feature films with country of origin and release year. Films released through 1975 are included in the text as are over 100 photographs. A very good source for individual credits up through the mid-1970s.

Parish, James Robert, and Don E. Stanke. The Debonairs. T. Allan Taylor, editor. New Rochelle, NY: Arlington House, 1975. 511p. $25.00. ISBN 0-87000-293-7.
Here is a work which covers the careers of several male film stars assoicated with sophisticated characterizations. Earl Anderson provides an interesting introduction followed

by essays and filmographies on George Brent, Melvyn Douglas, Cary Grant, Rex Harrison, Ray Milland, Robert Montgomery, David Niven, and William Powell. Like other biographical volumes of this kind, the book needs to be updated since all of its subjects are now deceased.

Parish, James Robert, and Leonard DeCarl. Hollywood Players: The Forties. New Rochelle, NY: Arlington House, 1976. 544p. il. $25.00. ISBN 0-87000-322-4.
Eighty-three popular film stars of the 1940s are covered in this coffee table volume which includes over 275 photographs. Concise, but informative, enteries for each star are followed by a listing of the person's films. Those included range from The Andrews Sisters, Diana Barrymore, Tom Conway, Sydney Greenstreet and Tom Neal, to Bill Elliott, Robert Paige, Patricia Morison, and Martha Vickers.

Parish, James Robert, and Don Stanke. Hollywood Baby Boomers: A Biographical Dictionary. New York: Garland, 1992. 670p. $75.00. ISBN 0-8240-6104-7.
Biographies, with filmographies, of dozens of movie stars born following World War II into the mid-1960s. Well researched and informative, the tome contains, among others, studies of Alec Baldwin, Kim Basinger, Sally Field, Mel Gibson, Arsenio Hall, Mark Harmon, Ann Jillian, Madonna, Bill Murray, John Ritter, Kurt Russell, Susan Sarandon, Cybill Shepherd, Sissy Spacek, Kathleen Turner, Ophrah Winfrey, and Debra Winger.
Parish, James Robert, Don E. Stanke, and Michael R. Pitts.

The All-Americans. New Rochelle, NY: Arlington House, 1977. 448p. il. $20.00. ISBN 0-87000-363-1.
Biographical essays and filmographies are provided for Gary Cooper, Henry Fonda, William Holden, Rock Hudson, Fred MacMurray, Ronald Reagan, and James Stewart. Nicely illustrated, the volume needs to be updated since most of its subjects are deceased and Reagan was elected president after the book's publication.

Peary, Danny. Cult Movie Stars. New York: Simon & Schuster, 1991. 608p. il. $35.00. ISBN 0-671-74924-2.
Fun look at over 750 film stars associated with cult followings. Illustrated with over 275 photos, the volume presents a thumbnail biography of each personality followed by a filmography which can include cult favorites, sleepers, and other key films. A conglomerate of screen personalities are included in this interesting outing.

Rainey, Buck. Heroes of the Range: Yesterday's Saturday
Matinee Movie Cowboys. Metuchen, NJ: Scarecrow Press,
1987. 366p. il. $37.50. ISBN 0-8108-1804-3.
A sequel to *Saddle Aces of the Cinema* (q.v.), this large
book provides biographies, filmographies and photographs of
Buddy Roosevelt, Tom Tyler, Bob Steele, Tim McCoy, Kermit
Maynard, George O'Brien, Tim Holt, Buster Crabbe, William
Boyd, Randolph Scott, Roy Rogers, Johnny Mack Brown,
Charles Starrett, Rod Cameron, and Jack Hoxie. Well researched.
Also published in a softbound edition (Waynesville, NC: The World
of Yesterday, 1987. 366p. $19.95 pap. ISBN 0-936505-03-6).

Rainey, Buck. Saddle Aces of the Cinema. San Diego,
CA: A.S. Barnes, 1980. 307p. il. $19.95. ISBN 0-498-02341-9.
Very readable series of biographies and filmographies of
popular cowboy film heroes. Those included are Roy Stewart,
Wally Wales, Tom Mix, Jack Perrin, Rex Bell, Harry Carey,
Buck Jones, Reb Russell, Al Hoxie, Ken Maynard, William
Duncan, Hoot Gibson, Gene Autry, Fred Thompson and Jack
Holt. This handsomely illustrated work was followed by a
sequel, *Heroes of the Range* (q.v.).

Rainey, Buck. Sweethearts of the Sage: Biographies and
Filmographies of 258 Actresses Appearing in Western Movies.
Jefferson, NC: McFarland, 1992. 632p. il. $95.00.
ISBN 0-89950-565-1.
A tremendous effort, this 8 1/2 x 11-inch hardbound volume provides
biographical sketches and film listings for actresses associated
with the western cinema. Nicely illustrated, the book is divided
into four parts, each dealing with different eras. The first
section covers the years up to 1920 with information on such
stars as Marguerite Clayton, Grace Cunard, Helen Gibson, Carol
Holloway, Winifred Kingston, Marin Sais, Nell Shipman, Blanche
Sweet, and Kathlyn Williams. Among the actresses of the 1920s
covered are Virginia Brown Faire, Carmelita Geraghty, Neva
Gerber, Josephine Hill, Eva and Jane Novak, Allene Ray, Alma
Rayford, and Fay Wray. By far the biggest section deals with
1930s and 1940s, the heyday of the "B" Western, and among the
feminine sagebrush players sketched are Jean Carmen, Phyllis
Coates, Penny Edwards, Dale Evans, Dorothy Fay, Jane Frazee,
Verna Hillie, Jennifer Holt, Anne Jeffreys, Mary Ellen Kay,
Fay McKenzie, Ruth Mix, Cecilia Parker, Marion Shilling, Peggy
Stewart, and Luana Walters. A final section deals with actresses
who were associated with big budget westerns, such as Julie Adams,
Yvonne De Carlo, Rhonda Fleming, Susan Hayward, Rita Hayworth,

Virginia Mayo, Maureen O'Hara, Vera Ralston, Jane Russell, Barbara Stanwyck, and Claire Trevor. Barbara Stanwyck did the Foreword for the volume and Charles Starrett provided a Tribute.

Rainey, Buck. Those Fabulous Serial Heroines: Their Lives and Films. Metuchen, NJ: Scarecrow Press, 1990. 537p. $59.50. ISBN 0-8108-1911-2.
Forty-six female stars of motion picture serials are covered in this large illustrated volume which also includes filmographies. The important silent screen pioneers like Pearl White, Ruth Roland, Allene Ray, Neva Gerber, and Juanita Hansen are included as are such sound era counterparts as Lucile Browne, Carol Forman, Lorna Gray (Adrian Booth), Jean Rogers, Linda Stirling, and Peggy Stewart. A treasure Trove for serial queen fans. Also published in a softbound Edition (Waynesville, NC: The World of Yesterday, 1990. 537p. $29.95 pap. ISBN 0-936505-10-9).

Rainey, Buck. Western Gunslingers in Fact and on Film. Jefferson, NC: McFarland, 1998. 341p. $35.00p. ISBN 0-7864-0396-9.
Attempting to separate and compare alleged historical fact and movie myth, the author presents coverage of seven wild west characters and gangs (Billy the Kid, The James-Younger Gang, The Dalton-Doolin Gang, Belle Starr, Wyatt Earp, Wild Bill Hickok, Bat Masterson). In each case a biographical sketch is presented followed by a list and discussion about the movies made portraying these characters. While the book makes it obvious that Hollywood has little use for historical fact, the volume is not only fun reading but also provides a useful reference source for its subjects. The book's bibliography is lengthy and of interest to historians.

Rothel, David. Those Great Cowboy Sidekicks. Metuchen, NJ: Scarecrow Press, 1984. 338p. $29.50. ISBN 0-8108-1707-1.
Thorough coverage of some thirty-nine movie cowboy sidekicks, this book gives emphasis to the major ones like Gabby Hayes, Smiley Burnette, Andy Devine, Al St. John, Max Terhune, Fuzzy Knight, and Pat Buttram. Biographies and filmographies for each player are provided as are a wealth of photographs. This volume will appeal to fans of cowboy movies.

Sennett, Ted. Masters of Menace: Greenstreet and Lorre. New York: E.P. Dutton, 1979. 228p. il. $8.95 pap. ISBN 0-525-47533-8.

The careers of two of the movies best villains, Sydney Greenstreet and Peter Lorre, are profiled in this volume which is highlighted by many illustrations. The book looks at the films the two actors did together as well as their individual careers. Filmographies for each are also included.

Shipman, David. The Great Movie Stars: The Golden Years. New York: Bonanza Books, 1970. 576p. il.
Large illustrated volume which provides well written profiles of scores of movie stars from the silent days into the 1940s. Following an interesting essay on the stars and the studio system, the author covers a variety of popular players, both from Hollywood and England. A unique book and one which more than fulfills its goal of being both informative and entertaining.

Slide, Anthony. The Vaudevillians: A Dictionary of Vaudeville Performers. Westport, CT: Arlington House, 1981. 178p. $19.95. ISBN 0-87000-492-1.
While basically a biographical study of dozens of famous vaudeville stars, this volume will appeal to film fans for the number of performers who also made movies. Among them are Abbott & Costello, Jack Benny, Fannie Brice, Burns & Allen, Eddie Cantor, Marie Dressler, Frank Fay, W.C. Fields, Ted Healy, Al Jolson, Harry Lauder, Ted Lewis, Nick Lucas, Marx Brothers, Ken Murray, Sally Rand, Harry Richman, Will Rogers, Chic Sale, Kate Smith, Fred Stone, Arthur Tracy, Ethel Waters, and Mae West.

Stewart, John. Filmarama, Volume 1: The Formidable Years, 1893-1919. Metuchen, NJ: Scarecrow Press, 1975. 401p. $15.00. ISBN 0-8108-0802-1.
Covering the cinema's early years, this book gives an alphabetical listing of performers and their screen credits along with birth and death dates, character names played if known and some stage credits. This is followed by a large index listing films in alphabetical order with release year and company and a cross reference to the performers. Now dated, this volume was a ground-breaking work at the time of its publication.

Stewart, John. Filmarama, Volume II: The Flaming Years 1920-1929. Metuchen, NJ: Scarecrow Press, 1977. 745p. $25.00. ISBN 0-8108-1008-5.
Done in the same format as the above volume, and the second but last work in a proposed series which would have

covered movies through 1969, this book covers the 1920s.
As expected it is much larger than the initial effort since
more films were made in the 1920s and more information on
them has survived. Again actors and their credits are listed in
the first section and then the movies are listed alphabetically
with a cross reference to the first section. As with Volume I,
this is a most useful research tool but one that has not aged.

Stuart, Ray. Immortals of the Screen. Los Angeles:
Sherbourne Press, 1965. 224p. il. $7.50.
Filled with over 600 stills, here is a coffee table volume which
provides biographical data on over 100 film stars. Unfortunately the
information given is not detailed or very reliable. Basically a curio.

Thompson, Frank T. Between Action and Cut: Five
American Directors. Metuchen, NJ: Scarecrow Press, 1985.
320p. $22.50. ISBN 0-8108-1744-6.
This is one of the best books to deal with film directors;
five of Hollywood's craftsmen are profiled in essays by
various writers. The directors covered are Victor Fleming,
Roland West, Charles Barton, Rowland Brown, and William K.
Howard. Each of the essays are thorough and well reserched
and a filmography with cast and credits is provided for each
director. All of the directors included are well covered, but
the most interesting pieces are Frank Thompson's article on
Charles Barton and Scott MacQueen's work on Roland West.

Twomey, Alfred E., and Arthur F. McClure. The Versatiles:
Supporting Character Players in the Cinema 1930-1955.
Cranbury, NJ, 1969. 304p. il. $10.00. ISBN 498-06792-0.
Thumbnail biographies and photographs are given for 400
actors and actresses who did character work in the first quarter
of a century of sound movies. The last part of the volume
lists another 200 performers with dates, photos, and brief film
lists. The book is best for including entertainers often
overlooked in other sources.

Wlaschin, Ken. The Illustrated Encyclopedia of the
World's Great Movie Stars and Their Films: From 1900
to Present Day. New York: Bonanza Books, 1979. 233p.
il. $24.95. ISBN 0-517-32123-8.
Illustrated with over 400 photos, this oversized volume
provides thumbnail biographies and best film listings for
hundreds of movie stars. Divided into the silent, classic
and modern eras, the book is informative and noteworthy
for the wide variety of subjects it includes.

Great Britain

Palmer, Scott. A Who's Who of British Film Actors.
Metuchen, NJ: Scarecrow Press, 1981. 561p. $27.50.
ISBN 0-8108-1388-2.
An alphabetical listing of film credits for more than 1,400
British performers, this volume is a fine research tool although
most of the personalities included are associated with the sound
era. For each actor, birth and death dates are given along with
a brief write- up followed by a chronological list of films and
their release years. Not only are major stars included but also
a large number of character performers. A very comprehensive
work.

BIOGRAPHICAL SOURCES--TELEVISION

General

Edgar, Kathleen J., ed. Contemporary Theatre, Film and Television: A
Biographical Guide Featuring Performers, Directors, Writers, Producers,
Designers, Managers, and Choreographers. Volume 20. Detroit, MI: Gale, 1998.
$151.00. ISBN 0787620580.

Gelbart, Larry, ed. Stand-Up Comedians on Television. Museum of Television and
Radio, 1996. il.
Profiles the medium's notable stand-up comics from the early years (e.g., Milton
Berle) to the present (e.g., Jay Leno, Jerry Seinfeld). The essays incorporate a wealth of
the standups' trademark routines, gags, stories, and patter and are complemented by more
than 125 photos.

Hill, George, Lorraine Raglin, Chas Floyd Johnson. Black Women in Television:
An Illustrated History and Bibliography. New York: Garland, 1990. (Garland
Reference Library of the Humanities, Volume 1228) il., bibl. ISBN 0824033396.
Documents the careers of notable black women involved--as actresses, singers,
directors, writers, and producers--in television series, special movies, soaps, and talk
shows between 1939-1989. Includes appendices listing Emmy, Oscar, and NAACP
Image award nominees and winners as well as series, films, and specials in which black
females had major roles.

Hilliard, Robert L., with Michael C. Keith. The Broadcast Century: A Biography
of American Broadcasting. 2nd ed. Focal Press, 1997. 320p. il. $39.95 pap. ISBN
0240802624.
Essentially a lively social history of the broadcast media, from the golden ages of
radio and television to the present day. Incorporates an ongoing timeline of world and

media events and 40 autobiographical sidebars from pivotal industry figures such as Steve Allen and Julia Child. The text is augmented by 200 illustrations, many of which are rare or previously unpublished.

O'Dell, Cary, and Sally J. Raphael. Women Pioneers in Television: Biographies of Fifteen Industry Leaders. Jefferson, NC: McFarland & Company, 1997. 264p. $59.00. ISBN 0786401672.

Reyes, Luis, and Peter Rubie. Hispanics in Hollywood: An Encyclopedia of Film and Television. New York: Garland, 1994. (Garland Reference Library of the Humanities, Volume 1761) il. $125.00. index, bibl. ISBN 0815308272.
The book is comprised largely of biographical sketches (performers and behind-thescene personnel) and description of films and TV programs that has a Hispanic characters, setting, or subject or in which a Hispanic actor starred. The program entries cite the producer, director, writer, cast, and a concise plot summary. Individuals highlighted by boldface type appear as the subject of biographical sketches in a later section of the work. Also includes essays regarding the role of Hispanic Americans in American film and television and a section with "profiles of selected non-Hispanic filmmakers who have contributed substantially to shaping the cinematic image of Hispanic Americans through classic films they made."

Slide, Anthony. Some Joe You Don't Know: An American Biographical Guide to 100 British Television Personalities. Westport, CT: Greenwood, 1996. 271p. il. index. $59.95. ISBN 0-313-29550-6.
Provides concise profiles of British performers appearing on U.S. television from the 1950s up to the present, most notably PBS stations, the Arts & Entertainment channel, and other cable networks recycling British shows. Each entry is appended with a listing of credits, along with dates and a bibliography. The index covers names of shows and actors who don't have a separate entry. Includes a survey of British programming in America, beginning in 1969 with the PBS broadcast of the *Forsyte Saga*.

Specific Individuals

--Brinkley, David

Brinkley, David. David Brinkley. Reprint ed. New York: Ballantine, 1996. il. $12.00 pap. ISBN 0345374029. Also available in audio cassette and large print editions.
Brinkley relates how a youth from a small southern town possessing a single onehundred-watt AM radio station evolved into one of the world's most respected broadcasters, most notably as co-host of the *Huntley-Brinkley Report* and anchor of Sunday morning's *This Week*. The work's strengths include his first-hand recollections of many of the great leaders of the twentieth century (e.g., Harry Truman, Winston Churchill, Lyndon Baines Johnson) and the early days of TV news, before live satellite feeds and videotape became commonplace--all presented in engaging fashion, punctuated by Brinkley's perceptive, dry wit.

--Diller, Barry

Mair, George. The Barry Diller Story: The Life and Times of America's Greatest Entertainment Mogul. John Wiley & Sons, 1998. 352p. il. $14.95. ISBN 0471299480.
The work focuses on Diller's triumphs; e.g., innovations such as the movie-of-theweek and the miniseries, programming coups at ABC, launching the Fox network, acquisition of the lucrative shopping network QVC. While successful in the delineation of television's business dealings, Mair is considerably less incisive in the portrayal of Diller's private life.

--Duchovny, David

Mitchell, Paul. The Duchovny Files: The Truth Is in Here. E C W Press, 1996. 284p. il., filmography. $16.95 pap. ISBN 1550222848.
An exhaustive compilation of bios and interviews centered around Duchovny, best known for hosting the cable series, *The Red Shoes Diaries*, and his starring role in *The X-Files*.
The text combines personal observations (e.g., family influences, his philosophy of acting) and pertinent factual data such as reviews of movies he has appeared in, available Internet resources, and plot summaries for his films and the first three seasons of *The X-Files*.

--Fuldheim, Dorothy

Mote, Patricia M. Dorothy Fuldheim; The First First Lady of Television News. Quixote Publications, 1997. 252p. il. $22.95. ISBN 0963308351.
The work surveys Fuldheim's personal life and career, most notably her publications and television interviews with many key figures of the mid-twentieth century. Mote pays particular attention to the forces behind Fuldheim's success during the infancy of the TV medium.

--Hickman, Dwayne

Hickman, Dwayne, and Joan Roberts Hickman. Forever Dobie: The Many Lives of Dwayne Hickman. Birch Lane Press, 1994. 301p. il. $19.95. ISBN 1559722525.
Hickman offers an engaging account of his acting career, most notably as a teen idol on *The Bob Cummings Show* and *Dobie Gillis*. While dishing up little dirt on his showbiz associates, he provides a wealth of background information as well as profiles of legendary figures like Cummings, Jack Benny, and Dobie Gillis creator, Max Schulman.

--Janssen, David

Janssen, Ellie, with J.D. Michael Phelps. David Janssen: My Fugitive. Lifetime Books, 1997. 180p. il. $14.95 pap. ISBN 0811908577. 1994 hardcover edition no longer in print.

A tell-all portrait of the star of television (*The Fugutive*; *Harry-O*; *Richard Diamond, Private Eye*) and film by his erstwhile wife. While noting Janssen's many problems (e.g., womanizing, bouts of heavy drinking, frequent unemployment), the book is sympathetic in approach, particularly its insightful discussion of the benefits and drawbacks of celebrity status.

--Letterman, David

Lefkowitz, Francis. David Letterman. Chelsea House, 1996. 127p. il. (Pop Culture Legends) $19.95 (library binding). ISBN 0791032523. Also available in paperback edition.
A succinct career account of the comedian, comedy writer, and late-night television show host. While offering little in the way of personal insights, the work chooses to focus instead on Letterman's professional challenges, most notably his competition with Jay Leno for hosting *The Tonight Show* as well as the subsequent ratings battle upon moving to CBS to anchor *The Late Show*.

--McMahon, Ed

McMahon, Ed, with David Fisher. For Laughing Out Loud: My Life and Good Times. Introduction by Johnny Carson. Warner Books, 1998. 355p. il. $23.00. ISBN 0446523704.
A breezy memoir, frequently punctuated by anecdotes and humorous asides, Revealing the fixture of *The Tonight Show* and *Star Search* (where he helped propel the likes of Rosie O'Donnell, Dennis Miller, LeAnn Rimes, and Sinbad to stardom) as well as countless ads and infomercials. McMahon argues that the key to his success is that he comes across as everyman. Despite his share of rough times, McMahon remains ever the optimist, thereby revealing a significant factor behind his popularity.

--O'Donnell, Rosie

Spreng, Patrick. Everything Rosie: The Ultimate Guide for Rosie O'Donnell Fans. Birch Lane Press, 1998. 224p. il. $19.95. ISBN 1559724528.
The biographical sections are supplemented by a profile of her online activities, addresses of her favorite charities, an introduction to members of her band--and their other accomplishments--and episode summaries of her talk show (featuring a list of the guests and memorable things they said and did).

--O'Sullivan, Terry

O'Sullivan, Terry. Did I Miss Anything?: Memoirs of a Soap Opera Star. Gaide Press, 1997. $16.95 pap. ISBN 1880090562.
In addition to profiling O'Sullivan's career as a television actor, the book provides a fascinating insider's look at the soap opera universe.

--Sherman, Bobby

Sherman, Bobby, with Dena Hill. Bobby Sherman: Still Remembering You.
NTC/Contemporary Publishing, 1996. 234p. il. $16.95 pap. ISBN 0809232065.
Sherman reminisces on his life, personal relationships, and career, from the television
debut on *Shindig* to the starring role on *Here Come the Brides*. The text is augmented by
over 100 high quality photos.

--Walters, Barbara

Remstein, Henna, and Martina S. Horner. Barbara Walters. Chelsea House, 1998.
112p. il. $19.95. ISBN 0791047164.
Geared to the young adult reader, the work provides an inspirational--albeit highly
informative--treatment of the television journalist whose interviewing skills have been
recognized by seven Emmy Awards.

BIOGRAPHIES/CAREER RETROSPECTIVES--FILM INDUSTRY

Ackerman, Forrest J. Lon of 1000 Faces! Beverly Hills, CA:
Morrison, Raven-Hill, 1983. 287p. $20.00 pap. ISBN
0-912-189-00-2.
Pictorial tribute to Lon Chaney Sr. with a few articles
added by his son, Robert Bloch, Ray Bradbury, Vincent Price,
and others. Although hardly an in-depth study, it is a pleasing
presentation of Chaney and his work except for the inclusion of
an endless series of puns.

Aherne, Brian. A Deadful Man: A Personal, Intimate
Book About George Sanders. New York: Simon and
Schuster, 1979. 224p. $9.95. ISBN 0-671-24797-2.
Actor Brian Aherne reminisces about his friend George
Sanders in this amusing, informative and ultimately touching
volume. Aherne recounts Sanders' marriages (he married two of
the Gabor sisters and found happiness with Ronald Colman's
widow, Benita Hume), his bizarre inventions and crazy financial
schemes, his long and successful film career and his ultimate
slide into ill health and depression which resulted in his
suicide. The authors lists the subject and Benita Hume as
assistants since many of their letters to him are reproduced in
the text.

Alyn, Kirk. A Job for Superman! Los Angeles: Kirk
Alyn, 1971. 118p. il.
Privately published memoirs of the first actor to portray
Superman on the screen. The author tells of his days as a

dancer on stage and with big bands and of his years in
Hollywood where he eventually became typed as a serial star.
Nicely illustrated and entertaining reading.

Anderson, Robert G. Faces, Forms, Films: The Artistry
of Lon Chaney. Cranbury, NJ: A.S. Barnes, 1971. 216p.
il. $8.50. ISBN 0-498-07726-8.
This heavily illustrated book covers the film career of
Lon Chaney, from his early stage years through being a bit
player in films to stardom. This films and characters are
discussed and a filmography is included. While not an in-depth
work, the volume does do a good job in outlining and discussing
Chaney and his career.

Anobile, Richard J., ed.. A Fine Mess!: Verbal and Visual
Gems from the Crazy World of Laurel and Hardy. New
York: Darien House, 1975. 256p. il. $9.95. ISBN
0-517-524-384.
A fun book which will delight Stan Laurel and Oliver Hardy
fans. The volume is made up of hundreds of frame enlargements
from Laurel and Hardy movies and shows the visual delights of
their work.

Astor, Mary. A Life on Film. New York: Delacorte Press,
1917. 245p. $7.50.
Having previously written her autobiography, *My Story*,
Mary Astor turns to discussing her more than one hundred
feature films in this informative and entertaining work. She
traces her beginnings in the silent era, her rise to stardom,
the coming of talkies, and her later years in character roles.
With candor, wit and intelligence, the actresses paints an
interesting picture of her life, profession, and co-workers.

Baker, Roger. Bette Davis: A Tribute 1908-1989. New
York: Gallery Books, 1989. 64p. il. ISBN 0-8317-0800-X.
A slim pictorial coverage of Bette Davis' film career. The
book adds nothing new about the star but many of the
photographs will fascinate her fans.

Barr, Charles. Laurel and Hardy. Berkeley, CA:
University of California Press, 1968. 144p. il. $1.95 pap.
The first appreciation of Stan Laurel and Oliver Hardy's films
in English, this volume covers the scope of their career from the
silent days, through their talkie classics and ending with *A Chump
at Oxford* (1940). Also provided is an interesting annotated
filmography and plenty of frame enlargements from their movies.

Bellamy, Madge. A Darling of the Twenties. Vestal, New
York: The Vestal Press, 1989. 202p. il. $12.95 pap. ISBN
0-911572-75-9.
Madge Bellamy was one of the most popular stars of the
1920s, appearing in such features as *Lorna Doone* (1922*), The
Iron Horse* (1924), *Lightnin'* (1925), *Sandy* (1926), *and The Play
Girl* (1928). Her story is somewhat typical: a beautiful and talented
young woman plagued by unhappiness, an overbearing mother, and
poor choices in husbands and boyfriends. Poor judgement caused
her to give up her career at the beginning of the sound era,
although she later attempted a comeback in "B" movies, including
the film for which she was best remembered, *White Zombie* (1932).
The last part of her book deals with failed comebacks and
matrimonial litigation. In an epilgoue she said she lived
in "abject povery for thirty- five years" but "I was not unhappy."
Madge Bellamy died at age 90, shortly after completing her life
story. This readable biography contains many photographs and
its covers reproduce color photos of Ms. Bellamy from fan
magazines. The book also has a useful filmography.

Belton, John. Robert Mitchum. New York: Pyramid
Publications, 1976. 159p. il. $1.75 pap.
A well done entry in the Pyramid Illustrated History of the
Movies series, this volume concentrates on the lengthy career
of Robert Mitchum. Mitchum's life, films, and screen persona
are nicely covered in this compact work, which also includes
diverse photos. Definitely a good read for Mitchum fans.

Billips, Connie. Janet Gaynor: A Bio-Bibliography.
Westport, CT: Greenwood Press, 1992. 155p. $35.00. ISBN
0-313-27574-2.
A fine entry in Greenwood Press' Bio-Bibliographies in the
Peforming Arts series, this volume is cheapened by the use of
cameraiready copy. Content-wise, the author has done a good
job chronicling the career of screen great Janet Gaynor.
Beginning with an informative biography, the book contains a
chronology, filmography, lists of radio, stage, and TV work, plus
a discography. A lengthy bibliography with nearly 700 entries
has also been provided.

Bogdanovich, Peter. Allan Dwan: The Last Pioneer. New
York: Praeger, 1971. 200p. $3.45 pap.
An appreciation of the lengthy film career of director
Allan Dwan which began in 1911 and concluded in 1961. The
book contains a long interview in which Dwan discusses

many of his films. It concludes with a thorough filmography. An important work on one of the cinema's best and most underrated directors.

Bogdanovich, Peter. John Ford. Berkeley, CA: University of California Press, 1968. 144p. $1.95 pap. John Ford discusses his career with Peter Bogdanovich in this combined series of interviews, which makes for good reading, especially for Ford followers. The volume also includes a useful filmography which begins with Ford's first film work in 1914 and concludes with *7 Women* in 1967.

Bojarski, Richard. The Films of Bela Lugosi. Secaucus, NJ: Citadel Press, 1980. 256p. il. $16.95. ISBN 0-8065-0716-0.
Top notch study of Bela Lugosi's films, plus an overall good review of his career in the entertainment medium. Following a lengthy biography, each of Lugosi's movies are covered with more emphasis given to sound era films. The actor's stage work from 1902 to 1956 is also denoted. In addition to the lucid text, the book is highlighted by hundreds of very interesting photographs. One of the best volumes in Citadel's long running series.

Bojarski, Richard, and Beale, Kenneth. The Films of Boris Karloff. Secaucus, NJ: Citadel Press, 1974. 287p. il. $12.00. ISBN 0-8065-0396-3.
Boris Karloff's long career as a cinematic boogey man is covered in the volume. Opening with a biographical chapter, the book looks at all of Karloff's films from 1919 to 1971, with more detail on his sound films than silent ones. Besides a fine array of photos, the book also lists Karloff's TV work from 1949 to 1969.

Bond, Johnny. Reflections: The Autobiography of Johnny Bond. Los Angeles: The John Edwards Memorial Foundation, 1976. 79p. il. $4.00.
Johnny Bond's brief autobiography not only covers his musical career but also his work in nearly forty films. Although short, the book contains much information including a detailed discography. It is also illustrated with photographs and newspaper clippings. A worthy addition to country music collections.

Bonomo, Joe. The Strongman. New York: Bonomo Studios, 1968. 352p. il. $7.95.

The autobiography of the world's strongest man, who also
had a career as a movie star and stuntman. Loaded with
photographs, this book traces Joe Bonomo's life and movie
career. Bonomo was also a physical culture expert and
wholesaler. Later issued in a softbound edition at $3.95.

Bordwell, David. The Films of Carl-Theodor Dreyer.
Berkeley, CA: University of California Press, 1981. 252p.
il. $11.95 pap. ISBN 0-520-04450-9.
More than 300 frame enlargements are used in this book
to illustrate the output of Danish director Carl-Theodor Dreyer,
whose classic works include *La Passion De Jeanne D'Arc*,
Vampyr, *Day of Wrath*, and *Order*. Dreyer's life, directorial
Techniques, and influence in the cinema world are discussed.
From his early silent efforts, each of his movies is dissected.
The volume also includes a biographical filmogrphy. An
In-depth study of an important European filmmaker.

Carman, Bob and Dan Scapperotti. The Western Films of
Sunset Carson. Lindenhurst, NY: Bob Carman, 1981. 72p.
il. $12.95 pap.
Following a biographical introduction, the starring westerns
of Sunset Carson are covered individually with lengthy plot
synopsis, cast, and credits. While the volume is handsomely
illustrated, there is no critical analysis of the movies.

Carone, James, and Larry Fine. Stroke of Luck. Hollywood,
CA: Siena Publishing, 1973. il. 293p.
Told in first person by Larry Fine of the Three Stooges,
this volume serves as the actor's autobiography. Fine recounts
his childhood as a violin prodigy, his eventual shift into
vaudeville, his teaming with Moe and Shemp Howard, and the
formation of the Three Stooges. The team's years with Ted
Healy are presented, as is their success with the addition
of Jerry "Curley" Howard and later Shemp's return, followed by
Joe Besser and Joe Da Rita. Fine touches often on his happy
family life, including his lenghty marriage to his wife Mabel.
A listing of the Three Stooges 216 movies is also provided.

Clarke, Robert and Tom Weaver. Robert Clarke: To "B"
Or Not To "B," A Film Actor's Odyssey. Baltimore, MD:
Midnight Marquee Press, 1996. 248p. il. $20.00 pap. ISBN
1-887664-02-5.
Robert Clarke recounts his long career in movies and TV
in this readable autobiography which is interspersed with some
interesting photographs. Clarke's career has run the gamut

from "A" productions to low grade schlock films, the latter
including his self-directed *The Hideous Sun-Demon* (1959).
The author tells a good story and the book makes for fun
reading. Suprisingly, the detailed filmography stops at 1965,
although Clarke has continued to make movies.

Cody, Iron Eyes, and Marietta Thompson. Iron Eyes Cody:
The Proud American. Madison, NC: Empire Publishing, 1988.
il. 142p. ISBN 0-944019-05-6.
Loaded with photographs, this biography relates the life
of Iron Eyes Cody, famed portrayer of Native Americans.
Not only does the book cover Cody's screen career, with a
filmography, but it also delves into his activities on behalf
of Native Americans.

Conway, Michael, Dion McGregor, and Mark Ricci. The
Films of Greta Garbo. New York: Citadel Press, 1965. 155p.
il. $5.95.
The first in Citadel Press' "The Films of . . ." series,
which set the style and standard for dozens of volumes to
follow. The book opens with Parker Tyler's essay on Garbo's
image and then each of her films is discussed with cast, credits,
plot synopsis, and reviews. Dozens of photographs are included.

Cremer, Robert. Lugosi: The Man Behind the Cape . Chicago:
Henry Regnery Company, 1976. 307p. $9.95. ISBN
0-8092-8137-6.
Informative biography of horror film star Bela Lugosi,
particularly good in tracing the actor's early years in
Hungary and Germany. The actor's work in Hollywood and
his medical drug addiction are also covered, as are his final
years working with Edward D. Wood Jr. A stageography and
filmography are also included.

Curtis, James. James Whale. Metuchen, NJ: Scarecrow
Press, 1982. 267p. $16.50. ISBN 0-8108-1561-3.
Knowlegeable account of the life of British film director
James Whale, who was responsible for such Universal classics
As *Frankenstein* (1931), *The Old Dark House* (1932), *The
Bride of Frankenstein* (1935), and *Show Boat* (1936). Using
archival sources, studio records, and interviews with those
close to Whale, both personally and professionally, the author
has devised a fine tribute to his subject.

De Carlo, Yvonne, with Doug Warren. Yvonne. New York:
St. Martin's Press, 1987. 264p. $17.95. ISBN 0-312-00217-3.

The autobiography of one of the screen's most beautiful
sirens, the volume details the life of the actress from her
early years in Canada through the tough times before she
reached stardom in the mid-1940s. She discusses her films,
lovers, children, and outlook on life. The author comes across as
an intelligent woman with a strong desire to succeed.

Dickens, Homer. The Films of Marlene Dietrich. New
York: Citadel Press, 1968. 223p. il. $7.95.
Another well researched entry in Citadel Press' "The Films
of . . " series, this book covers the career of glamour queen
Marlene Dietrich from her earliest German movies of the 1920s
into the 1960s. The author provides cast, credits, plots, and
notes on each movie and the book is loaded with stills not
only from the films, but also candids and stage shots.

Di Franco, J. Philip. The Movie World of Roger Corman.
New York: Chelsea House, 1979. 237p. il. $11.95 pap. ISBN
0-87754-122-1.
One of the first volumes to cover the career of prolific
producer-director-distributor Roger Corman, the book contains
an interview with the subject and his co-workers, and then briefly
discusses each of his motion pictures. The highlight of the book
is its many illustrations, including a superb color section of
poster reproductions. Now out of date, the volume provides
useful coverage of Corman's career through the 1970s.

Everson, William K. The Films of Laurel & Hardy.
New York: Citadel Press, 1967. 223p. il. $6.95.
Following brief biographies of its two subjects, this
book covers all the short and feature films of the movies
most famous comedy team, Stan Laurel and Oliver Hardy.
The author provides lucid text along with brief credits and
a variety of photographs.

Eyles, Allen. John Wayne and the Movies. South
Brunswick, NJ: A.S. Barnes, 1976. 320p. il. $15.00.
ISBN 0-498-0149-5.
One of the better works on the career of John Wayne, this
one is solely dedicated to covering his many film appearances
and does so in fine form. After brief introductory essays,
including one by Louise Brooks, the volume studies Wayne's
films beginning in 1926 and going through the next half-century.
Each movie is discussed, the essays varying in length according
to the importance of the film and its impact on the subject's
career. For example, Wayne's early work is lumped into short

chapters, such as the one covering the sixteen westerns he did for Paul Malvern's Lone Star Productions between 1933 and 1935. Individual films are not given their own chapters until *Stagecoach* in 1939, and by that time Duke had been a star for nearly a decade. In discussing the individual features, the author provides not only plot synopsis, but a succinct overview of each title. The volume also contains a lengthy filmography and is well illustrated.

Fernett, Gene. Starring John Wayne. Cocoa, FL:
Brevard, 1970. 189p. $7.95.
Except for a brief epilog by Olive Carey, this picture book of John Wayne's film credits has nothing to recommend it. Not only is the book incomplete, it contains little information on the star's career, with mostly uncaptioned pictures. It is also laced with errors. The information for the 1935 feature *The New Frontier* is actually from the film of the same title from 1939, although the latter is not included under that title or its TV moniker *Frontier Horizon*. Wayne is also listed as starring in the 1936 feature *The Three Musketeers*, a film in which he did not appear. Suprisingly this volume, the epitome of shoddy research and tacky production, was reissued in a updated, albeit equally slapdash, paperback.

Fowler, Karin J. David Niven: A Bio-Bibliography.
Westport, CT: Greenwood Press, 1995. 299p. $59.95. ISBN
0-313-28044-4.
A fine addition to Greenwood Press' generally excellent Bio-Bibliographies in the Performing Arts series, this volume thoroughly covers the career of David Niven. It contains a biography, filmography, lists of stage and radio productions, discography, television appearances, books by the subject, his awards, and an extensive bibliography.

Fraser, Harry L. I Went That-A-Way: The Memoirs of a Western Film Director. Metuchen, NJ: Scarecrow Press, 1990. 161p. $25.00. ISBN 0-8108-2340-3.
Pleasant and informative reading is provided by this brief biography from veteran poverty row director and writer Harry L. Fraser. The author discusses how he made films at the lowest depths of Hollywood's poverty row for little money and lots of tenacity. Starting in the silent days, the author discusses working with stars like Gene Autry, Frank Buck, Harry Carey, Ray Corrigan, Hoot Gibson, Buck Jones, Ken Maynard, Ruth Mix, Rex Bell, and John Wayne as well as such producers as Louis Weiss and Trem Carr. His most amusing story tells of cowboy star Bill Cody mounting a horse backwards.

Graham, Cooper C., Steven Higgins, Elaine Mancini, and Joao Luiz Vieira. D.W. Griffith and the Biograph Company. Metuchen, NJ: Scarecrow Press, 1985. 343p. $27.50. ISBN 0-8108-1806-X.
More than 800 Biograph movies directed and/or supervised by D.W. Griffith from 1908 to 1913 are detailed in this book. Cast and credits for each films is provided, as are filmograpies for studio players. A very thorough and valuable research tool for those interested in the cinema's early years.

Grey, Rudolph. Nightmare of Ecstasy: The Life and Art of Edward D. Wood Jr. Los Angeles: Feral House, 1992. 232p. il. $14.95 pap. ISBN 0-922915-04-0.
The cult movie favorite *Ed Wood* (1994) was based on this oral history of the movies and career of schlock film maker Edward D. Wood Jr. The volume is filled with fascinating stories and photographs, although it fails to give the full story of its subject. In addition, biographical notes are given for the contributors, a chronology of Wood's life is included, as is a filmography, a list of unrealized projects and a bibliography of his books. The latter, suprisingly, does not include his best known work, *The Pearl Hart Story* (1962).

Griffis, Ken. Hear My Song: The Story of the Celebrated Sons of the Pioneers. Los Angeles: The John Edwards Memorial Foundation, 1977. 149p. il. (JEMF Special Series, No. 5). $6.26 pap.
The story of the most famous western singing group, The Sons of the Pioneers, is given in this work which also includes photographs and a lengthy discography plus a listing of the group's numerous film appearances and details of their song books. Griffis does a good job presenting the history of the Pioneers, whose original members included Leonard Slye (later Roy Rogers), Bob Nolan, Tim Spencer, and brothers Hugh and Karl Farr. Later members (i.e., Lloyd Perryman, Tommy Doss, Ken Carson, Rusty Richards) are also profiled and a list of the compositions of Bob Nolan and Tim Spencer are also provided. This is a very thorough history of the Sons of the Pioneers up to the time of publication, although it needs updating since the group is still active.

Grupenhoff, Richard. The Black Valentino: The Stage and Screen Career of Lorenzo Tucker. Metuchen, NJ: Scarecrow Press, 1988. 202p. $22.50. ISBN 0-8108-2078-1.

Black film star Lorenzo Tucker (1907-86) is profiled in
this thin volume which studies both his stage and movie careers.
Tucker is best known for starring in all-black films made by
Oscar Micheaux and the background of those movies is presented
here, as are a number of interesting stills and poster reproductions.
A well- written biography of one of the cinema's lesser
known stars.

Henderson, Robert M. D.W. Griffith: The Biograph Years.
New York: Farrar, Straus & Giroux, 1970. 250p. $2.95 pap.
ISBN 374-5-0958-1.
The nearly 500 films made by D.W. Griffith at the Biograph
Studios from 1908 to 1913 are detailed in this volume. The
book looks at Griffith's early days at Biograph, the move to
Cuddebackville in 1909 and California the next year, and the
emergence of the two reeler and longer efforts. Also discussed
is Griffith's work with cameraman Billy Bitzer and his relationship
with his stock company which included his wife, Linda
Arvidson. A filmography and a players' listing are included.

Howard, Moe. Moe Howard and the Three Stooges.
Secaucus, NJ: Citadel Press, 1977. 208p. $14.00. ISBN
0-8065-0554-0.
In this pictorial autobiography, Moe Howard recounts
his long career in show business and the story behind the
comedy team the Three Stooges. Howard gives a fascinating
glimpse behind the scenes in the history of the famous
comedy trio, which not only included Moe and Larry Fine
but also Moe's brothers, Curley and Shemp, as well as Joe
Besser and Joe Da Rita. A must for Three Stooges fans.

Jensen, Paul M. The Cinema of Fritz Lang. New York:
A.S. Barnes, 1969. 223p. $2.95 pap. ISBN 498-07415-8.
Very informative study of the career of German director
Fritz Lang, including work in his homeland on films like *Dr.
Mabuse* (1922), *Siegfried* (1924), *Metropolis* (1926), and *M*
(1931). Much attentio n is given to his Hollywood years and
such movies as *Fury* (1936), *The Return of Frank James* (1940),
Ministry of Fear (1944), *Clash By Night* (1952), *Human Desire*
(1954), and *While the City Sleeps* (1956). A primer for anyone
interested in the cinematic work of Fritz Lang.

Kaminsky, Stuart M. Don Siegel: Director. New York:
Curtis Books, 1974. 319p. $1.50 pap.
An important work detailing the films of director Don
Siegel, whose features included *Private Hell 36* (1954),

Invasion of the Body Snatchers (1956), *The Lineup* (1958),
Flaming Star (1960), *The Killers* (1964), *Coogan's Bluff*
(1969), *The Beguiled* (1971), and *Dirty Harry* (1971).
The author discusses Siegel's life and films, and includes
an interview with the subject in addition to a detailed
filmography. A well done book which should be updated
to include Siegel's later work, such as *The Shootist* (1976).

Konow, David. Schlock-O-Rama: The Films of Al
Adamson. Los Angeles: Lone Eagle Books, 1998. 160p.
il. $19.95 pap. ISBN 1-58065-001-5.
A tribute to schlock movie director Al Adamson, who
was murdered in 1995. Chocked full of photos and poster
reproductions, the work covers such reverse classics as
Dracula vs. Frankenstein, Horror of the Blood Monsters,
Blood of Ghastly Horror (which had a metamorphosis from
Psycho-A-Go-Go), and *Five Bloody Graves*. Each film is
discussed at length and a filmography is provided. Also
devotes space to Adamson's wife and co-star, the late
Regina Carrol, and Independent International Pictures
(a studio which he co-owned). A treasure trove for Al
Adamson fans.

Koszarski, Diane Kaiser. The Complete Films of
William S. Hart: A Pictorial Record. New York: Dover,
1980. 151p. il. $8.95 pap. ISBN 0-486-23863-6.
Although subtitled "A Pictorial Record," coverage of
all of William S. Hart's movies is done much more in-depth
than merely presenting illustrations. While the more than
250 photos in the volume are memorable, each of the star's
films is also covered with cast and credits, plot synopsis, and
critical reviews. The opening chapter covering Hart's life
and career is very well written and perceptive. Hart's film
career lasted from 1914 to 1925, and he eschewed talkies
except for the prologue to the 1939 reissue of his final
feature, *Tumbleweeds*.

Lee, Raymond. The Films of Mary Pickford. South
Brunswick, NJ: A.S. Barnes, 1970. 175p. il. $8.95.
Anemic look at Mary Pickford's movie career which
mainly contains a picture gallery of her work. The slim
volume opens with an essay on the Pickford mistique and
concludes with a list of her movies, but the bulk of the
work is a large number of stills from various Pickford
productions.

Lenning, Arthur. The Count: The Life and Films of
Bela "Dracula" Lugosi. New York: G.P. Putman's Sons,
1974. 347p. il. $10.00. ISBN 399-11340-1.
Loaded with illustrations, this biography of Bela Lugosi
was written by a fan of the actor's who met him when he was
a child. The author presents an entertaining and informative
look at the Hungarian actor and how he became typed as Count
Dracula and the star of horror movies, although his roots were
in the classical stage. A filmography is also provided.

MacGillivray, Scott. Laurel & Hardy: From the
Forties Forward. Lanham, MD: Vestal Press, 1998.
224p. $19.95p. ISBN 1-879511-35-5.
Following a brief foreword by Steve Allen, the author
provides extended coverage of the careers of Stan Laurel and
Oliver Hardy, including a detailed account of their neglected
1940s films and their work in radio and on stage. The volume
provides a wealth of information and proves the comedy duo
was still productive and popular in the twilight of their
careers. Also covered is the marketing of Laurel and Hardy
films, various compilation features, and the revival of the
boys on video. Surprisingly the various Laurel and Hardy
recordings (they had a charted single in England in the 1960s)
are not discussed. A fine addition to the literature on the
movies' most popular comedy team.

Maltin, Leonard. The Disney Films. New York: Crown,
1973. 312p. il. $9.95. ISBN 0-517-500469.
A tribute, as well as a history, of Walt Disney's feature
films is presented in this nicely illustrated volume. Following
an interesting essay on the background of the Disney studio,
the author discusses each of the company's movies providing
cast, credits, plot, and interesting comments. This book will
be highly valued by Walt Disney fans. A third edition of the
book was published in 1995 (New York: Hyperion, 1995.
384p. $16.95 pap. ISBN 0-7868-8137-2).

Maltin, Leonard, ed. The Laurel and Hardy Book.
New York: Curtis Books, 1973. 301p. il. $1.50 pap.
Fun potpourri about the careers of Stan Laurel and Oliver
Hardy, including personal reminiscences, critical essays,
career studies of co-stars, lists of their films separately, and a
very thorough filmography of their films together (compiled
by Richard W. Bann). Filled with nice illustrations, the
volume is informative and fun to read.

Marrill, Alvin H. The Films of Anthony Quinn.
Secaucus, NJ: Citadel Press, 1975. 256p. il. $12.00.
ISBN 0-8095-0470-6.
This book opens with a biographical chapter on Anthony
Quinn; it then proceeds to detail each of his film appearances
from 1936 to 1974, with cast, credits, plots, and analysis,
along with scores of pictures. Also included is a list of
Quinn's stage and TV appearances. One of the better entries
in Citadel's "The Films of . . " series.

Marrill, Alvin H. Samuel Goldwyn Presents. Cranbury,
NJ: A.S. Barnes, 1976. 320p. il. $19.95. ISBN
0-498-01658-7.
All of the feature films produced by Samuel Goldwyn
between 1923 and 1959 are presented in this book with
cast, credits, plots, and analysis. The volume opens with
a brief chapter on Goldwyn's life and career, and also
includes a list of radio and TV adaptations of his films.
Loaded with illustrations, this work is a fine tribute to its
subject.

Martin, Tony, and Cyd Charisse. The Two of Us.
New York: Mason/Charter, 1976. 286p. $12.50. ISBN
0-88405-363-6.
As told to Dick Kleiner, this combined autobiography
of Tony Martin and Cyd Charisse will appeal to their fans.
The long- married couple talk about their life stories in
separate chapters. Tony tells of his rise to stardom in
music and movies, his harrowing World War II experiences,
and the major stardom that came from clubs, records, and TV
in the 1940s, 1950s, and 1960s. Cyd discusses her life-long
love of dancing, her first marriage to Nico Charisse, and
her successful movie career. Both discuss their successful
marriage and their stage partnership.

Matthews, Jessie. Over My Shoulder: An Autobiography.
New Rochelle, NY: Arlington House, 1974. 240p. $8.95.
ISBN 0-87000-311-9.
A touching and very candid autobiography by British stage
and film star Jessi Matthews, who recounts her rise from the
chorus in the 1920s to near international stardom in the next
decade followed by years spent struggling with mental illness.
The contrasting highs and lows of her career make for good
reading, most notably the relationship with husband Sonnie
Hale, who eventually left her for a younger woman.

McCabe, John, Al Kilgore, and Richard W. Bann. Laurel and Hardy. New York: Ballantine Books, 1976. 400p. il. $6.95 pap. ISBN 0-25127-X-695.
A tome to be treasured by all Stan Laurel and Oliver Hardy fans, this book contains hundreds of still photographs from the duo's many films, compiled by Al Kilgore with intelligent and informative text by John McCabe and thorough filmographies by Richard W. Bann. This may well be the best book ever written about Laurel and Hardy and it is certainly the most fun.

McCarty, Clifford. Bogey: The Films of Humphrey Bogart Secacus, NJ: Citadel Press, 1965. 191p. il. $5.95.
One of the earlier enteries in Citadel's "The Films of . . ." series, this volume opens with a short biographical introduction and then covers Humphrey Bogart's movie appearances in chronological order. Laced with lots of photographs, the book gives each film's cast and credits along with a plot synopsis, but without comments. Best for beginning Bogart fans.

McCoy, Tim, with Ronald McCoy. Tim McCoy Remembers. Garden City, NY: Doubleday, 1977. 274p. $8.95. ISBN 0-385-12798-7.
Cowboy star Tim McCoy spins many an intriguing yarn in this educational autobiography, which has its emphasis on his experiences in the West and with Native Americans. McCoy also talks about his years in Hollywood, his successful last marriage, and his later years touring with Tommy Scott's medicine show.

McGee, Mark Thomas. Roger Corman: The Best of the Cheap. Jefferson, NC: McFarland, 1988. 261p. $32.50. ISBN 0-89950-330-6.
An affectionate look at the film career of producer-director Corman, from his salad days with American International Pictures through his Edgar Allan Poe films with that company and his later establishment of his own company, New World. The book also includes a filmography of the movies directed by Corman, biographies of his "stock company" of players, and a list of the movies he produced but did not direct.

Moshier, W. Franklyn. The Alice Faye Movie Book. Harrisburg, PA: Stackpole Books, 1974. 194p. il. $9.95. ISBN 0-8117-0086-0.
A fan's tribute to his favorite actress, this volume nicely details the movie career one of the most popular performers of the 1930s and 1940s, Alice Faye. The author begins the

book with a biographical overview of the actress' life and career, followed by a look at her individual films in the style of Citadel's "The Films of . . ." series. Each title is covered with cast and credits, plot synopsis and a discussion, augmented by a representative selection of photographs. A brief discography is also included. The tome was later updated as *The Films of Alice Faye*.

Mulholland, Jim. The Abbott and Costello Book. New York: Popular Library, 1975. 254p. il. $3.95 pap. ISBN 445-08372-395.
The careers of Bud Abbott and Lou Costello are thoroughly covered in this oversized softbound volume which will delight fans of the comedy duo. Although the main emphasis of the book is given to the coverage of the team's films, other areas of their activities are also highlighted, such as Broadway, radio, and television. Indexes for both their films and TV shows are also included. The volume contains many interesting photographs.

Nareau, Bob. The 'Real' Bob Steele and a Man Called 'Brad'. Mesa, AZ: Da'kine Publishing, 1991. 156p. $15.00 pap.
Thorough research highlights this book which delves into the life and career of cowboy star Bob Steele. The author uncovers the facts behind the actor's life including much information about his father, director Robert North Bradbury, and his twin brother, Dr. William Bradbury. A book to be valued by Bob Steele fans.

Parfitt, Gary. The Films of Peter Cushing. Bath, England: HFCGB Publishers, 1975. 92p. $7.00 pap.
Short, but useful, tribute to horror film star Peter Cushing. The softbound book contains evaluations of the actor and his career, an interview, a list of his movies, and a portrait gallery. Director Terence Fisher provides the introduction among those providing brief tributes are Vincent Price, Veronica Carlson, Robert Quarry, and Denis Gifford.

Parish, James Robert, with Whitney, Steven. The George Raft Story. New York: Drake Publishers, 1973. 288p. il. $7.95. ISBN 0-87749-520-3.
Unauthorized biography of movie tough guy George Raft, from his days as a dancer and pal of gangsters to movie stardom and public notoriety. The first half of the book is a biography and the last part is an in-depth look at his movies with cast, credits, plots, and analysis. Listings of Raft's radio and TV work are also provided.

Parish, James Robert, and Whitney, Steven. Vincent Price
Unmasked. New York: Drake Publishers, 1974. 265p. $9.95.
ISBN 0-87749-667-6.
Biographical coverage of Vincent Price's lengthy career
is provided in this well researched book. The study of Price's
life and career takes up the first part of the volume with the
rest divided into sections listing his stage, films, radio and
TV work, and his writings.

Pastos, Spero. Pin-Up: The Tragedy of Betty Grable.
New York: G.P. Putnam's Sons, 1986. 175p. $16.95.
ISBN 0-399-13189-2.
Although she was the G.I.'s number one pinup of World
War II and the biggest box office draw of that time, Betty
Grable lead an essentially unhappy life according to this
well researched biography. Detailed is her sad childhood,
rise to stardom, unsuccessful marriages to Jackie Coogan
and Harry James, her lovers, and her failures as a parent.
Her last years were spent working to pay off ex-husband
Harry James' gambling debts, even while she was suffering
from cancer.

Pierce, James H. The Battle of Hollywood. House of
Greystoke, 1978. il.
Privately published autobiogaphy of James H. Pierce, the
Indiana boy who grew up to play Tarzan in *Tarzan and the
Golden Lion* (1927) and on radio, and who married Joan
Burroughs, the daughter of Tarzan's creator, Edgar Rice
Burroughs. A filmography, photo section, and various letters
are also included.

Pohle, Robert W. Jr., and Douglas C. Hart. The Films
of Christopher Lee. Metuchen, NJ: Scarecrow Press,
1983. 305p. $32.50. ISBN 0-8108-1573-7.
One of the better efforts to chronicle a film career, this
work on Christopher Lee is greatly enhanced by the participation
of its subject, who often provides illuminating comments on his
various movies as well as an informative foreword. Lee's movies
from 1947 through the early 1980s are covered in detail and
the book provides a wealth of information on the subject's
career. Another asset is the inclusion of dozens of stills
in the center of the book. Lee's radio and television work
is also examined. This fine work is in need of updating in that
the subject has done more than twenty films, as well as a compact
disc, since its publication.

Quirk, Lawrence J. The Films of Gloria Swanson. Secaucus, NJ: Citadel Press, 1984. 256p. il. $14.95 pap. ISBN 0-8065-1077-3.
Well done biographical and pictorial study of the movies of Gloria Swanson, who the New York Times called "The greatest star of them all." Following an essay on her lengthy career, each of the star's films from 1915 to 1974 are covered with cast, credits, and analysis. Many interesting stills also highlight the work.

Quirk, Lawrence J. The Films of Joan Crawford. Secaucus, NJ: Citadel Press, 1968. 222p. il. $7.95. ISBN 0-8065-0008-5.
Another in Citadel Press' lengthy "The Films of. . " series, this volume covers the work of Joan Crawford, a major star for over a half century. As with the previous vo lumes in the series, the book contains a long biographical introduction followed by a discussion of each of Joan Crawford's films from 1925 to 1968. Cast and credits, plot synopsis, critical reviews, and stills are provided for each title.

Rainey, Buck. The Fabulous Holts. Nashville, TN: WFC Press, 1976. 216p. il.
Biographies of Jack Holt and his two children, Tim and Jennifer Holt, both of whom also became stars. All three are associated with westerns and their films are covered in this heavily illustrated book. Filmographies for all three are also provided.

Rainey, Buck. The Life and Times of Buck Jones: The Silent. Waynesville, NC: World of Yesterday, 1988. 263p. il. $14.95 pap. ISBN 0-936505-07-9.
Buck Jones was one of the silent era's most popular cowboy heroes and his life and films through 1928 are detailed in this well researched volume. Loaded with pictures, the book covers the subject's early years, his supporting parts in movies, and stardom at Fox. Each film includes cast, credits, plot, and a critical review. The book ends with the failure of his own production, *The Big Hop* (1928), and the brief run of his wild west show. A bibliography is also included.

Rainey, Buck. The Life and Films of Buck Jones: The Sound. Waynesville, NC: World of Yesterday, 1991. 388p. il. $24.95 pap. ISBN 0-936505-08-07.
A follow-up to the above work, this book covers the life and films of Buck Jones from 1929 until his tragic death in

1942. Like the previous book, each of the subject's films are covered with cast, credits, plot, and critical reviews. There are also chapters on the Buck Jones Rangers, biographies of Jones' leading ladies, an addendum to the initial volume, and a lengthy bibliography. Like the first work, this one also includes hundreds of photographs.

Ralston, Esther. Some Day We'll Laugh: An Autobiography. Metuchen, NJ: Scarecrow Press, 1985. 244p. $16.00. ISBN 0-8108-1814-0.
The entertaining autobiography of silent screen beauty Esther Ralston, whose career faded with the coming of sound but who kept acting well into the 1960s. The actress talks about working with directors Josef von Sternberg and Dorothy Arzner as well as such leading men as Gary Cooper, Richard Arlen, and Richard Dix. Among the films she discusses are *Peter Pan* (1924), *A Kiss for Cinderella* (1926), *The Case of Lena Smith* (1929), and *Rome Express* (1933).

Rhodes, Gary Don. Lugosi: His Life in Films, on Stage, and in the Hearts of Horror Lovers. Jefferson, NC: McFarland, 1997. 430p. il. $55.00. ISBN 0-7864-0257.
Bela Lugosi's life and career is given thorough coverage in this extremely detailed work. Thanks to his cult status, Bela Lugosi is more famous than ever, and this volume attempts to fill in the details of his long and highly interesting career. Not only are all of the actor's many films covered but so are his numerous stage appearances, radio, television and vaudeville work, plus other activities such as his Las Vegas revue and his appearances with spook shows. A fairly thorough bibliography is included, as is a discussion of the merchandising of Lugosi and his image. The only thing missing appears to be a section on his recordings. While more of a scrapbook than a biography, the volume will delight Bela Lugosi fans.

Ricci, Mark, Boris Zmijewsky, and Steve Zmijewsky. Films of John Wayne. New York: Citadel Press, 1970. 288p. $5.95. ISBN 0-8065-0222-3.
One of the first books to cover John Wayne's film career, this volume is a typical entry in Citadel's "The Films of . . ." series. It opens with a biographical essay on the star and then gives individual coverage to each of his films appearances, beginning with *Mother Machree* in 1928 (he actually started doing bits two years earlier) and continues through *Rio Lobo* (1970). The book was later updated to include all of

Wayne's films through *The Shootist*, his final feature, in 1976.
Although somewhat perfunctory, the volume does a fair job
in rounding up information on John Wayne's feature films.

Ringgold, Gene, and DeWitt Bodeen. The Complete Films
of Cecil B. DeMille. Secaucus, NJ: Citadel Press, 1969. 377p.
il. $12.95 pap. ISBN 0-8065-0956-2.
Almost as grandiose as one of his film spectaculars, this
tome covers all of the movies of producer-director Cecil
B. DeMille from *The Sqauaw Man* in 1914 to *The Ten
Commandments* in 1956, with cast, credits, story, and reviews.
The work includes a listing of the "Lux Radio Theatre"
episodes hosted by DeMille.

Ringgold, Gene. The Films of Bette Davis. New York:
Citadel Press, 1966. 191p. il. $6.95.
Bette Davis's film career is covered from 1931 to 1965 with
only perfunctory mention of her pre-film stage work and a
foreword by Henry Hart. Heavily illustrated, the book lists
Davis' films chronologically with cast, credits, plot synopsis,
and selected critical reviews.

Ringgold, Gene. The Films of Rita Hayworth: The
Legend and Career of a Love Goddess. Secaucus, NJ:
Citadel Press, 1974. 256p. il. $12.00. ISBN
0-8065-0439-0.
Probably the best entry in Citadel's "The Films of . . "
series, this book gives thorough and loving coverage to the
life and career of Rita Hayworth. The author has done a
superb job in not only covering all of the star's movies,
but he also provides an indepth biographical study of the
Love Goddess. While the movies are covered in the usual
Citadel series manner, the author gives a more personal touch
to the essays, giving the plots briefly in deference to
critical anaylsis, the latter supplemented by quotes from
various contemporary reviewers. Highlighted by scores of
photographs, the volume also contains a list of the star's
television appearances and unrealized film and stage projects.

Rothel, David. The Gene Autry Book. Waynesville, NC:
The World of Yesterday, 1986. 326p. il. $12.95 pap. ISBN
0-936505-04-4.
A potpourri of information about Gene Autry is provided
in this large softbound volume which contains many pictures.
Included is Autry trivia, little known facts about the star,
his wit and wisdom, discography, filmography, a list of his

TV shows, collecting Autry memorabilia, and magazine article reprints. A treasure trove for Gene Autry fans.

Rothel, David. The Roy Rogers Book. Madison, NC: Empire Publishing, 1987. 223p. il. $25.00 pap. ISBN 0-944019-01-3.
Like the author's *The Gene Autry Book* (q.v.), this work contains a conglomerate of information about Roy Rogers and will appeal to his many fans. It contains an interview with the subject, Roy Rogers trivia and little known facts, his wit and wisdom, discography, filmography, TV log, and collecting Rogers memorabilia. Full of photos, the book is an appealing one and a must for Rogers followers.

Scagnett, Jack. The Laurel & Hardy Scrapbook. Middle Village, New York: Jonathan David Publishers, 1976. 160p. il. $12.95. ISBN 0-8246-0207-2.
An affectionate look at the movies of Stan Laurel and Oliver Hardy, told in terms of their lives rather than delving into their films. Although it contains a brief filmography, the book's chief interest is its many photographs, some of which are candid shots.

Schelly, William. Harry Langdon. Metuchen, NJ: Scarecrow Press, 1982. 249p. $16.00. ISBN 0-8108-1567-2.
Harry Langdon was considered one of the silent screen's great comedians, in league with Charlie Chaplin, Buster Keaton, and Harold Lloyd. Through his own doing and because of changing public taste he had a quick fall from major stardom, but as this book points out he remained active and successful until his death in 1944. This biography follows the comedian from his days in medicine shows to films with Mack Sennett and stardom in the mid-1920s. In the sound era he starred mainly in short subjects and also provided material for a half dozen feature films in which he did not appear, including several Laurel and Hardy movies. This book sets the record straight on the Little Elf and is a fine biography of a screen immortal.

Shrum, Cal. The Cal Shrum Story. Springfield, IL: Cal Shrum, 1986. 71p. il. $12.95 pap.
There is not much to be found in this cheap looking selfpublished autobiography by country-western musician and film actor Cal Shrum. About the only interest are some photographs from Shrum's career and his brief comments on the starring westerns he did in New Mexico around 1950. This booklet has little to offer, even for fans of the writer.

Svehla, Gary J., and Svehla, Susan, ed. Bela Lugosi.
Baltimore, MD: Midnight Marquee Press, 1995. 312p. $20.00
pap. ISBN 1-887664-01-7.
Cult star Bela Lugosi is profiled in this volume, the
initial entry in the Midnight Marquee Actors Series. Through
the discussion of several of his movies the actor's life,
acting style, and screen persona are brought forth. Among the
movies dissected by various writers are *Dracula, Murders at
the Rue Morgue, White Zombie, The Black Cat* (1934), *The
Raven, Dark Eyes of London, Son of Frankenstein,
Frankenstein Meets the Wolfman, Return of the Vampire,*
and *Bride of the Monster*. A filmography is also included,
as are essays on Lugosi and his work with Edward D. Wood Jr.
A fine tribute to Lugosi.

Svehla, Gary J., and Susan Svehla, editors. Boris Karloff.
Baltimore, MD: Midnight Marquee Press, 1996. 384p. $25.00
pap. ISBN 1-887664-07-6.
Thirty-two of Boris Karloff's feature films are analyzed
in this volume by various writers. They include *Frankenstein,
The Mask of Fu Manchu, The Mummy, The Old Dark House,
The Black Cat, The Lost Patrol, Bride of Fankenstein, The
Walking Dead, Before I Hang, The Body Snatcher, Comedy of
Terrors,* and *Targets*. Also discussed is the stage production
Arsenic and Old Lace and a complete filmography is provided.

Svehla, Gary J., and Susan Svehla, editors. Lon Chaney Jr.
Baltimore, MD: Midnight Marquee Press, 1997. 360p. $20.00
pap. ISBN 1-887664-15-7.
An actor of considerable depth and power, Lon Chaney Jr.
is spotlighted in this informative volume through the discussion of
more than two dozen of his films, his contribution to the western
genre and an episode of the "Route 66" TV show in which he
recreated some of his famous monster roles. Among the films
profiled are *Of Mice and Men, The Wolfman*, the Mummy series,
the Inner Sanctum series, *High Noon, Big House U.S.A., The
Alligator People, Witchcraft,* and *SpiderBaby*. A useful
filmography is included, but a chapter comparing Chaney to
other genre players seems unnecessary.

Taylor, Jackie Lynn. The Turned-On Hollywood 7:
Jackie Remembers Our Gang. Toluca Lake, CA: Pacifica
House, 1970. ISBN 911098-15-1.
Collaborating with her husband Jack Fries, Jackie Lynn
Taylor wrote this spiral bound pictorial guide to the "Our Gang"

comedies in which she once appeared. With a foreword by Art Linkletter and comments by Hal Roach and Jackie Cooper, the book is at best a perfunctory guide to the ageless series. Its best section provides biographical information on other series players like Dickie Moore, Johnny Downs, Allen "Farina" Hoskins, Matthew "Stymie" Beard, Darla Hood, Carl "Alfalfa" Switzer, and George "Spanky" McFarland. Also included is a update on the author's career since her "Our Gang" days.

Thomas, Tony, Rudy Behlmer, and Clifford McCarthy. Films of Errol Flynn. New York: Citadel Press, 1969. 221p. $8.95.
Following a foreword by Greer Garson and an essay on the subject's early years, the authors discuss each of Errol Flynn's movies from *In the Wake of the Bounty* (1933) to *Cuban Rebel Girls* (1959), including such classics as *Captain Blood, The Adventures of Robin Hood, Dodge City, Dive Bomber, Gentleman Jim, Objective Burma, Adventures of Don Juan*, and *The Sun Also Rises*. Although the text is more brief than many volumes in the Citadel series it also tends to be more informative.

Thompson, Frank T. William A. Wellman. Metuchen, NJ: Scarecrow Press, 1983. 339p . $22.50. ISBN 0-81-8-1594-X.
A definitive study of the work of director William A. Wellman, which included such classics as *Wigs, The Public Enemy, A Star Is Born, Nothing Sacred, Beau Geste, The High and the Mighty*, and the autobiographical *Lafayette Escadrille*. Biograpical information is also provided as is a detailed filmography.

Thornton, Chuck, and David Rothel. Allan "Rocky" Lane: Republic's Action Ace. Madison, NC: Empire Publishing, 1990. 181p. il. $20.00. ISBN 0-944919-09-9.
Biography of western film star Allan Lane which emphasizes his starring work at Republic Pictures. Each of his many cowboys movies are covered with cast, credits, and plots. In addition there is a discussion and listing of his other movies, including serials, his being the voice of "Mr. Ed" on TV, comments by his co-workers, the Rocky Lane comics, and the reproduction of several magazine articles about the star. Filled with photos, the book will be a must for fans of the subject.

Thornton, Chuck, and David Rothel. Lash LaRue: The King of the Bullwhip. Madison, NC: Empire Publishing, 1986. 160p. il. $20.00. ISBN 0-944010-06-4.

Lash LaRue's western movie career is given thorough
coverage in this volume which opens with a poem by its
subject followed by a biographical essay. After that comes
a lengthy interview with LaRue. Each of his starring westerns
is covered with a detailed plot synopsis, cast, and credits.
The book is loaded with photos, some from LaRue's collection.
Also included are his last starring movies in the 1980s, *The
Dark Power* and *Alien Outlaw*.

Tuska, Jon. The Films of Mae West. Secaucus, NJ:
Citadel Press, 1973. 191p. il. $12.00. ISBN 0-8065-0377-7.
Fairly good coverage of Mae West's movies is provided
in this entry in Citadel Press' "The Films of . . ." series.
Laced with photographs and providing cast and credits, each
of the star's movies are thoroughly discussed, although the
book came out before the release of her final movie,
Sextette in 1977. Quite a bit of space is given to stage
credits as well.

Ursini, James. Preston Sturges: An American Dreamer.
New York: Curtis Books, 1973. 240p. $1.50 pap.
Useful career study of writer-producer-director Preston
Sturges who went from playwright and scripter to become one
of Hollywood's most successful directors before a quick slide
into oblivion. The volume recounts Sturges' life, hits like
The Great McGinty, *Sullivan's Travels*, *The Palm Beach Story,
as well as* such flops as *Mad Wednesday* and *The Beautiful
Blonde From Bashful Bend*.

Van Hise, James, Edward Wagenknecht, and Anthony Slide.
The Films of D.W. Griffith. New York: Crown, 1975. 276p. il.
$12.95. ISBN 0-517-523264.
A superb study of the feature films of D.W. Griffith
which nicely mixes lucid text and interesting photographs.
The first chapter summarizes Griffith's Biograph short films
and then each of his feature length movies is covered
individually with cast, credits, plot synopsis, and critical
analysis. A must for anyone interested in Griffith's career.

Vermilye, Jerry. Bette Davis. New York: Pyramid
Publications, 1973. 159p. il. $1.45 pap. ISBN
0-515-02932-7.
Compact but useful coverage of the film career of
Bette Davis, from 1931 into the early 1970s. Davis' many
films are covered in an entertaining fashion, and the book
includes numerous photographs and a filmography. Another

good entry in the Pyramid Illustrated History of the Movies series.

Walker, Alexander. Joan Crawford: The Ultimate Star. New York: Harper & Row, 1983. 192p. il. $29.95. ISBN 0-06-015123-4.
Authorized by Metro-Goldwyn-Mayer, this biography of glamour queen Joan Crawford is both a loving tribute and a critical study of the actress. Handsomely illustrated with more than 250 photographs, the book covers Crawford's life and career and is both informative and fun reading. A brief filmography is also provided.

Wayne, Jane Ellen. Crawford's Men. New York: Prentice Hall, 1988. 256p. il. $16.95. ISBN 0-13-188665-7.
By its title, this book appears to be an intimate look into Joan Crawford's love life; instead, it is a more than serviceable biography. The book is filled with quotes, both from the subject and those around her, and it also contains a nice selection of photographs.

Whisler, John A. Elvis Presley: Reference Guide and Discography. Metuchen, NJ: Scarecrow Press, 1981. 265p. $14.50. ISBN 0-8108-1434-X.
Hundreds of magazine and newspaper articles about Elvis Presley are chronicled in this volume, along with an extensive discography. Books about Presley are also included, as is a song title index and an extensive general index. A must for Elvis Presley researchers.

Williams, Lucy Chase. The Complete Films of Vincent Price. New York: Citadel Press, 1995. 287p. il. $19.95 pap. ISBN 0-8065-1600-3.
A superb accounting of Vincent Price's long film career with thorough coverage given to each of his movies, including informative commentary by the author. A lengthy biographical sketch opens the work, which includes an introduction by the subject written in 1959. This well illustrated volume is a fine tribute to Price and his 100 film appearances.

Wray, Fay. On the Other Hand. London: Weidenfeld & Nicolson, 1990. 270p. il. ISBN 0-297-81108-8.
Fay Wray began appearing in films in the mid-1920s as a teenager and became famous as the movies' first "scream queen" in King Kong in 1933. In this candid and entertaining autobiography, the actress recounts her more than 75 films,

her marriages and children, and how she survived Hollywood
to be one of its keenest observers. A delightful screen memoir.

CATALOGS/UNION LISTS--FILM INDUSTRY

Brady, Anna. Union List of Film Periodicals: Holdings of
Selected American Collections. Westport, CT: Greenwood,
1984. 31p. Title change and geographical indexes. ISBN
0-313-23702-6.
The listing, including more than 1,000 film-related periodicals
arranged alphabetically by title, distinguishes between open and
closed publications, title variations, and complete, partial, or
broken runs. The main text is supplemented by sections explaining
how to use the tool and how to identify participating libraries and
their respective *National Union Catalog* codes.

Gartenberg, Jon, with others, eds. The Film Catalog: A
List of Holdings in the Museum of Modern Art. Boston: G.K.
Hall, 1985. 443p. il., index, filmog. ISBN 0-8161-0443-3.
MOMA's compute-generated catalog includes about 5,500 titles,
ranging from fiction and documentaries to television commercials
and home movies. Alphabetically arranged by title (except when
more apropriate to employ type, such as newsreel, or descriptive
title, such as "screen test" designations), the entries cite title,
alternate title, date, country, classification, producer or production
company, director, and museum film number. The producer and
director index assists greatly in accessing the catalog. The
appended filmography is arranged in chronological order.

Matzek, Richard A., comp. Directory of Archival Collections
on the History of Film in the United States. For the Audiovisual
Committee, Resources and Technical Services Division, Association
of College and Research Libraries On-Line Audiovisual Catalogers.
Chicago: Resources and Technical Services Division, American
Library Association, 1983. [46p.] pap.
The monograph delineates fifty-six U.S. archival collections concerned with
movie history. Arranged by state and institution, it provides information on
services, restrictions, and times open to the public. An appendix indicates
the location of archival resources relating to twenty-four studios.

CATALOGS/UNION LISTS--TELEVISION

Black, Sharon, and Elizabeth Sue Moersh, eds. Index to the Annenberg Television
Script Archive: Volume 1, 1976-1977. Phoenix, AZ: Oryx, 1990. 206p. author and
subject indexes. ISBN 0-89774-553-1.
The work encompasses 2,477 archived prime-time television scripts aired on the
major networks during the 1976-1977 period. Entries are organized alphabetically by

title; each includes draft date, script date, date aired, subject covered, famous people as characters, time, adaptation source, author, title, pagination, and notes. Other strong points include a lucidly written introduction (explaining access strategies) as well as the striking typography and layout design.

Godfrey, Donald G., comp. Reruns on File: A Guide to Electronic Media Archives. Hillsdale, NJ: Lawrence Erlbaum, 1992. 322p. program and subject indexes. $65.95; $29.95 pap. ISBN 0-8058-1146-X; 0-8058-1147-8 pap.
The source provides an inventory of institutional holdings--libraries, archives, and commercial distributors--based in thirty-nine states, the District of Columbia (considerable space is given over to the vast array of Library of Congress collections), Canada, and the United Kingdom. The entries, arranged alphabetically by state and followed by Canada and the U.K., include program typology and subject coverage, special interests, accessibility, location, and contact information. A wide range of formats are represented, from cylinders to compact discs for audio and virtually every conceivable type of video storage. The main text is complemented by a concise survey of recorded sound history and a section illustrating approaches to the location of broadcast archive materials.

Rouse, Sarah, and Katharine Loughney, comps. 3 Decades of Television: A Catalog of Television Programs Acquired by the Library of Congress, 1949-1979. Washington, D.C.: Motion Picture, Broadcasting, and Recorded Sound Division, Library of Congress, 1989. 688p. il. genre/format index. ISBN 0-8444-0544-2.
This tool compiles 1,400-odd television programs acquired by the Library of Congress that were commercially released between 1949 and 1979. Arranged alphabetically by title, the entries cite copyright, production company, date, telecast data, condition of copy, shelf number, cast, credits, synopses, and format and content/genre descriptors.

Shamley, Sarah L., comp. Television Interviews, 1951-1955: A Catalog of Longines Chronoscope Interviews in the National Archives. National Archives Trust Fund Board, 1991. $25.00. ISBN 0911333827.

COLLECTOR AND PRICE GUIDES--TELEVISION

General

Cain, Dana, and Diana Cain. Collecting Monsters of Film and TV: Identification & Value Guide. Iola, WI: Krause Publications, 1998. 192p. il. $22.95 pap. ISBN 0873415159.
This visually arresting work concentrates on the memorabilia depicting classic characters of the cinematic horror genre. Through continued TV showings and spinoff programs, monsters such as Frankenstein and King Kong are as well known to present day couch potatoes as they were to the filmgoers of yesteryear. Each entry delineates a particular monster and provides a selective listing of souvenirs along with estimated price valuations based on documented transactions with the collectibles marketplace.

Davis Greg, and Bill Morgan. Collector's Guide to TV Memorabilia, 1960s & 1970s. Paducah, KY: Collector Books, 1996. 277p. il., index. $24.95. ISBN 0-89145-705-4.

The tool provides suggested price valuations for a wide range of merchandise tied to television programs whose original network run took place--at least in part--between 1960-1979. Comprised of forty-six entries (each of which focuses on a particular show), the text is arranged in alphabetical order, beginning with *The Beverly Hillbillies* through *Wonder Woman*. The entries include an opening section providing information about the program (e.g., series time frame, number of episodes, ratings data, characters and regular performers), color photographs, and an inventory of memorabilia. Among the produc ts cited are toys, games, kitchenware, print materials, posters, school resources, and other collectibles identified with a particular show.

Davis, Greg, and Bill Morgan. Collector's Guide to TV Toys and Memorabilia: 1960s & 1970s. 2nd ed. Paducah, KY: Collector Books, 1999. 320p. il., index. $24.95. ISBN 1574320947.

This edition represents a substantial expansion of the 1996 publication. The authors have documented over 1,700 additional collectibles, 2,300 in all depicted by 1,300 color photos. The entries--more than fifty overall--now include, in addition to pertinent program information, general descriptions of the collectibles and information regarding mail order and Internet collecting. Also includes a foreword by Erin Murphy, the actress playing Tabitha on *Bewitched*.

Durbal, Bryan, and Glen Bubenheimer. Vintage Televisions: Identification & Values. Collector Books, 1999. 176p. il. $19.95 pap. ISBN 1574321269.

The authors, both collectors of TVs, claim this is "the most comprehensive vintage television guide available." It lists more than 1,400 entries of all makes and models of post-World War II televisions; the entries include up-to-date "real- world pricing" and a multitude of photos to aid in identification.

Hake, Theodore L. Hake's Price Guide to Character Toy Premiums: Including Premiums, Comic, Cereal, TV, Movies, Radio and Related Store Bought Items. 2d ed. New York: Avon, 1998. 624p. il. $24.95 pap. ISBN 0380800764.

While television program characters constitute only a portion of the items included in the source, they are nevertheless well represented. The entries include product descriptions, photos, and price valuations.

Longest, David. Cartoon Toys & Collectibles Identification and Value Guide. Collector Books, 1998. 224p. $19.95 pap. ISBN 1574320750.

The scope of this guide reaches far beyond television to include animation artifacts in media such as motion pictures, newspapers, comic books and sound recordings. However, many of the cartoon characters depicted here have appeared on the tube, whether through primetime or Saturday morning TV series (e.g., *The Flintstones* and countless other Hanna-Barbera creations), syndication broadcasts of cinematic works (e.g., the original Popeye cartoons), and media tie-ins like *The Archies*.

Individual Programs and Celebrities

--Ball, Lucille

Wyman, Ric B. For the Love of Lucy: The Complete Guide for Collectors and
Fans. Abbeville, 1995. il. $35.00. ISBN 0789200066.
The work is divided between the presentation of career data and the listing of related
memorabilia. Presents an exhaustive filmography as well as radio and television credits'
including the title of each episode of the five series starring Ball and the original
broadcast date. The text is greatly enhanced by 624 illustrations (392 in color), most of
which depict Lucille Ball collectibles such as comic books, fanzines, *TV Guide* covers, *I
Love Lucy* pajamas, board games, paper dolls, movie posters, collector's plates, cigar
bands, and advertisements.

--*The Long Ranger*

Felbinger, Lee J. Collector's Reference & Value Guide to the Lone Ranger.
Collector Books, 1998. 144p. il. $18.95. ISBN 57432022X.
The source includes a selective inventory of souvenirs and other merchandise
associated with the western hero in some of his notable media permutations; e.g., radio,
television, comic books and pulp digests. The abundance of photographs assist the text
immeasurably in describing the listed items.

--*Star Trek*

Snyder, Jeffrey B. A Trekker's Guide to Collectibles: With Values. Schiffer
Publishing, 1996. 160p. $29.95 pap. ISBN 0887409652.
A selective listing of products depicting characters and props from the 1960s cult TV
series. Entries, arranged by topic, include descriptive details, photographs, and price
valuations.

DICTIONARIES--FILM INDUSTRY

Konigsberg, Ira. The Complete Film Dictionary. New York:
New American Library, 1987. 420p. il. ISBN 0-453-00564-0;
0-452-00980-4 pap.
The tool's more than 3,500 entries address all elements of the
film industry, including technology, production, film making,
distribution, economics, history, and criticism. The text is
enhanced by line drawings and motion-picture stills.

Naha, Ed. The Science Fictionary: An A-Z Guide to the
Worlds of SF Authors, Films & TV Shows. Wideview Books,
1980. 388p. $10.95 pap. ISBN 0-87223-629-3.

Science fiction authors, films and TV programs are detailed
in this volume which contains over 1,000 entries. Films and
TV shows are discussed and cast, credits and plots interpolated.
Biographical sketches are also supplied for a number of genre
authors. This volume covers the best to the worst of sci- fi and
does so in an informative way.

Singleton, Ralph S. Filmmaker's Dictionary. Beverly Hills,
CA: Lone Eagle, 1986. 188p. ISBN 0-943728-08-8.
The source defines the 1,500 technical terms, slang, and expressions
most "widely- used" within the film ad television industry. The
definitions are first rate, and many other useful features can be
found (for example, words defined elsewhere in the dictionary
are placed in caps); however, Konigsberg's *The Complete Film
Dictionary* provides more exhaustive coverage of the field.

Slide, Anthony. The American Film Industry: A Historical
Dictionary. Westport, CT: Greenwood, 1986. 431p. index,
bibl. ISBN 0-313-24693-9.
This thorough and lucidly written work contains more than
600 entries delineating producing and releasing companies,
technological innovations, film series, genres, organizations,
and technical terms.

Thomas, Nicholas, ed. International Dictionary of Films and
Films and Filmmakers. [Volume] 1: Films. 2nd ed. Chicago:
St. James Press, 1990. 1105p. bibl. ISBN 1-55862-037-0.

Thomas, Nicholas, ed. International Dictionary of Films
and Films and Filmmakers. Volume 2: Directors. 2nd ed.
Chicago: St. James Press, 1991. 958p. bibl., filmog. ISBN
1-55862-038-9.
Volume 1 covers 650-odd films (arranged alphabetically by
Title). The entries are divided into three parts: production
Details, a bibliography of published editions of the script and
Commentaries in periodicals and books, and a critical essay.
Volume 2 is composed of 480 alphabetically arranged
entries that focus on the primary themes exhibited by
the output of each respective director.

DICTIONARIES--TELEVISION

Bianculli, David. Dictionary of Teleliteracy: Television's 500 Biggest Hits, Misses,
and Events. New York: Continuum Publishing Company, 1996. 416p. il. index. ISBN
0-8264-0577-0.

Defining teleliteracy as "fluency in the language and content of TV," Bianculli--a New York-based TV journalist and reviewer--explores the medium on several fronts: as art form, cultural influence, and common language. Arranged alphabetically by program title, the text focuses on those programs felt by the author to have made a significant contribution to the development of the medium. A historical outline, notable trivia, and overall assessment are provided for each show.

Ensign, Lynne Naylor, and Robin Eileen Knapton. The Complete Dictionary of Television and Film. Briarcliff Manor, NY: Stein and Day, 1985. 256p. ISBN 0-8128-2922-0.
The terminology (general, technical, jargon, and slang) of the television and film industries is covered in more than 3,000 entries, arranged alphabetically and spanning both older and contemporary words and phrases.

Miller, Carolyn Handler. Illustrated T.V. Dictionary. New York: Harvey House, 1980. 135p. ISBN 0-8178-6220-X.
Following a concise introductory survey of television history and technology, Miller brings together technical and common usage terms as well as key performers, developers, innovators, and programs in a work geared to the uniformed layperson. Although dated, the work remains useful as a general guide to the medium.

Reed, Robert M., and Maxine K. Reed. The Facts on File Dictionary of Television, Cable, and Video. New York: Facts on File, 1994. 226p. ISBN 0-8160-2947-4.
The work consists of concisely defined terms--alphabetically arranged from A.C. Nielsen Company to zoom lens--concerned with the electronic visual media past and present. Ten specific topics are addressed by the entries: advertising, agencies/associations/companies/unions, broadcasting/cablecasting, educational/corporate communications, engineering, general terms and processes,government/legal, home video, production, and programming.

Slide, Anthony. The Television Industry: A Historical Dictionary. Westport, CN: Greenwood, 1991. Ix, 374p. name and program indexes. $59.50. ISBN 0-313-25634-9.
The tool's more than 1,000 entries--concerned with production companies, organizations, distributors, technical terms, popular jargon, and stylistic genres, and thematic material (e.g., racism)--focus on the American television industry, information on the international scene is also well represented. Includes a general bibliography of reference books on television; a substantial number of the individual topics also have incorporated a list of key readings. The appendix provides biographical surveys of three key figures in the development of the medium: ABC's Leonard H. Goldenson, CBS's William S. Paley, and NBC's David Sarnoff.

DIRECTORIES--FILM INDUSTRY

Singer, Michael, comp. and ed. Michael Singer's Film Directors: A Complete Guide. 9th ed. Beverly Hills, CA: Lone Eagle, 1992. 560p. il., index. ISBN 0-943728-46-0.

The tool includes more than 2,500 directors, noting nationalities, birthdates, films, and business addresses both for directors and their agents.

DIRECTORIES--TELEVISION

AV Market Place 1998: The Complete Business Directory of Products & Services for the Audio Video Industry Including: Audio, Audio Visual, Computers. 26th ed. New York: Bowker, 1998. $206.25. ISBN 0835239292.

Hollywood Reporter. 1998 Blu-Book Film and TV Production Directory. VerDugo Press, 1998. 500p. $69.95 pap. ISBN 0941140229.
Provides a comprehensive listing of entities involved in television and motion picture production. The alphabetically arranged entries include addresses and phone numbers.

Pintoff, Ernest. The Complete Guide to American Film Schools and Cinema and Television Courses. New York: Penguin USA, 1994. 510p. $17.95 pap. ISBN 0140172262.
While not an all- inclusive listing (institutions offering a few film or TV courses as opposed to a full- fledged degree program are generally not cited), the work should prove useful for prospective students and faculty as well as researchers attempting to identify those schools known for their film and television resources.

Television Directors Guide, compiled and edited by Lynne Naylor. Beverly Hills, CA: Lone Eagle, c1990- . Annual. film title index.
Alphabetically arranged listing of directors for network, cable, and syndicated programs--comedy series, drama series, variety series, specials, and pilots--broadcast in prime time. Each entry cites contact name and telephone number in addition to program credits. Also includes Emmy Awards and nominations section, a breakdown of programs by genre, and a directory of agents and managers.

Television Writers Guide, edited by Lynne Naylor. Beverly Hills, CA: Lone Eagle, 1989- . Annual.
The work--arranged alphabetically by writer--utilizes the same format as Naylor's *Television Directors Guide*.

ENCYCLOPEDIAS--FILM INDUSTRY

Bucher, Felix. Germany. London: A. Zwemmer, 1970. 298p. $3.50 pap. ISBN 498-075176-6.
A part of Tantivy Press' Screen Series, this volume is an illustrated guide to more than 400 actors, directors, writers, technicians and others in the German cinema. It is cross-referenced with an index of over 6,000 titles. A superb research tool.

Cawkwell, Tim, and Smith, John M., ed. The World
Encyclopedia of the Film. New York: World Publishing, 1972.
444p. $25.00. ISBN 0-529-04815-9.
One of the first, and better, attempts to cover world cinema in an
English language work, an international reference guide with over
2,000 enteries and 500 hundred photographs covering a multitude
of actors, directors, writers and other technicians. The work
concludes with a huge index which is really a filmography of
the thousands of international titles covered in the text.

Fernett, Gene. American Film Studios: An Historical
Encyclopedia. Jefferson, NC: McFarland, 1988. 295p.
$35.00. ISBN 0-89950-250-4.
A compilation of magazine pieces, this illustrated volume
covers the histories of various film studios, with an emphasis
on the silent era. Among the sixty-five companies chronicled
are American Mutoscope and Biograph, Balboa Studios, Chaplin
Studios, Columbia, Larry Darmour Studio, Essanay, Grand
National, Lubin, Nestor, Pathe, Charles Ray Studios, Hal
Roach, Mack Sennett, Thanhouser, and Vitagraph. While this
may be the author's best work it still should not be used as
a reference source without seeking other collaboration.

Hardy, Phil, ed. The Encyclopedia of Horror Movies.
New York: Harper & Row, 1986. 408p. il. $34.50. ISBN
0-06-055050-3.
A grandiose look more than 1,300 horror films from the
cinema's infancy into the early 1980s, this heavily illustrated
volume is a must for fans of the genre. Hardy and contributors
Tom Milne, Paul Willemen, Verina Glaessner, Julian Petley, and
Tim Pulleine provide consise but thorough coverage for all the
films included and the scope of the book is worldwide. One of
the best books written to date on horror movies. Overlook Press
updated the volume in the 1990s.

Hardy, Phil. The Film Encyclopedia: Science Fiction. New
York: William Morrow, 1984. 400p. il. $25.00. ISBN
0-688-00842-9.
Beginning in 1895 and going to 1983, this book thoroughly
covers over 1,200 science fiction movies and includes some 450
photographs from the Kobal Collection. In addition to author
Hardy, contributions to the text were also made by Denis Gifford,
Anthony Masters, Paul Taylor, and Paul Willemen. Like the above
work, this volume represents a momumental coverage of its genre
and it is one which sci- fi fans will treasure.

Hardy, Phil. The Film Encyclopedia: The Western.
New York: William Morrow, 1983. 402p. il. $25.00. ISBN
0-688-00946-8.
Perhaps the least satisfying of author Hardy's oversized
hardback series on various film genres, *The Western* nonetheless
is a major effort in the coverage of sagebrush sagas. Limited
to the sound era, the covers not only big budget efforts but
also a number of "B" westerns. As ususal, Hardy's text is crisp
and to the point and his insights meaningful. The heaviest
illustrated of the series, it contains over 650 photographs.
There is also an appendix listing hundreds of titles not
included due to space limitations.

Hogan, David J. Who's Who of the Horrors and Other
Fantasy. San Diego, CA: A.S. Barnes, 1980. 279p. il.
$19.95. ISBN 0-498-02475-X.
Subtitled "The International Personality Encyclopedia of
the Fantastic Film," this coffee table volume covers over one
thousand people involved with the horror, science fiction and
fantasy film fields. Each entry provides birth and death
dates, a thumbnail account of the person's involvement in
the genres and a list of their films in these areas with year
of release. While the bulk of the enteries are for performers,
many producers, directors, writers, camera people, special
effects artists, makeup artists and other technicians are
included. The volume is well illustrated and contains a
listing of genre movies by year from 1896 through 1981.

Maltin, Leonard. Leonard Maltin's Movie Encyclopedia.
New York: Dutton, 1994. 976p. il. $34.95. ISBN
0-525-93635-1.
More than 2,000 actors and filmmakers from the past and
present are given career profiles in this hefty volume. The
author's writeups are interesting and informative and the book
will be especially valuable for beginning researchers. There
are problems, however, especially with selection since the
work includes Charlie Korsmo and Ione Skye but not Francis X.
Bushman or Ramon Novarro. Also most of Charles Bronson's
1990s films are not listed and Frances Farmer's "briefly hosted"
Indianapolis TV show actually ran for six years.

Naha, Ed. Horrors: From Screen to Scream. New York:
Flare/Avon, 1975. 306p. il. $4.95 pap. ISBN 0-380-00499-2.
An encyclopedia listing hundreds of horror, science fiction
and fantasy films from 1910 to the mid-1970s, this volume covers

a great deal of material in a workmanlike fashion. For each
film its years of release and company are given as is a brief
writeup that includes listing stars and sometimes directors.
It also contains many photographs although most are familiar.
A pretty good compilation which is adequate for research into
the mid-1970s.

Weldon, Michael J. The Psychotronic Encyclopedia of Film.
New York: Ballantine Books, 1983. 813p. il. $16.95 pap.
ISBN 0-345-30381-4.
A fun and informative loving look at over 3,000 films
which can be called culturally ambivalent. Not only are the
reviews interesting and informative but they are just as fun
as their subjects. Nicely illustrated, this work helped
begin a wave of appreciation of low budget movies, both of the
past and present. Charles Beesley, Bob Martin, and Akira Fitton
also provided some of the reviews. This volume is a must for
anyone who loves offbeat cinema.

ENCYCLOPEDIAS--TELEVISION

General

Betancourt, John Gregory, and Roger Fulcon. The Sci-Fi Channel Encyclopedia of
TV Science Fiction. New York: Warner Books, 1998. 656p. 2 photo inserts. $15.99
pap. ISBN 0446674788.
The work includes virtually every science fiction series broadcast on television since
the late 1940s. The entries, arranged alphabetically by program title, provide basic series
and cast information.

Deandrea, William L. Encyclopedia Mysteriosa: A Comprehensive Guide to the
Art of Detection in Print, Film, Radio, and Television. New York: Macmillan, 1997.
405p. $26.00 pap. ISBN 0028616782.
The work offers over 1,400 entries--arranged alphabetically with extensive
crossreferences--
covering writer biographies, notable characters, and important works. The
text is enhanced by essays on key topics by experts, an appendix citing directories of
relevant organizations and major award winners, and a glossary of terms. Deandrea,
recently deceased, authored mystery and suspense novels, and was a regular columnist
for the respected journal, *The Armchair Detective*. He won a third Edgar Award for this
reference tool.

Hyatt, Wesley. The Encyclopedia of Daytime Television: Everything You Ever
Wanted to Know About Daytime TV But Didn't Know Where to Look! Watson-
Guptill, 1997. 528p. $24.95. il. ISBN 082308312.

An alphabetically arranged listing of all series broadcast for three or more weeks on a commercial network between 1947-1996 in addition to 100 nationally syndicated programs from the same five-decade time frame. The entries--which include soap operas, women's series, game shows, live sports, cartoons, and children's fare-- indicate length of program run, principal cast members, and key developments. The text is complemented by over 100 photographs.

Murray, Michael D., ed. Encyclopedia of Television News. Phoenix, AZ: Oryx, 1998. 320p. $69.00. ISBN 1573561088.
The more than 300 alphabetically arranged entries concentrate on broadcast journalists who have made a notable impact regarding particular news specialties, key stories, or important insights or coverage (e.g., Tom Brokaw, Katie Couric, Walter Cronkite, Linda Ellerbee, Fred Friendly, Ted Koppel, Charles Kuralt, Cokie Roberts). Also includes behind-the-scenes industry professionals who've generated important ideas or played a key role in program development as well as topical headings relating to news management and other specialty fields (e.g., documentary and public affairs programming). At the time of publication, Murray was chairman of the Department of Communication, University of Missouri, St. Louis. Over 100 television news experts contributed signed articles to the work.

Newcomb, Horace, Cary O'Dell, and Noelle Watson, editors. Encyclopedia of Television. 3 Volumes. Fitzroy Dearborn, 1997. 2,200p. il. $300.00 (library binding). ISBN 1884964265.
An exhaustive treatment of the medium which covers programming, notable personnel, and concepts. Entries are arranged alphabetically and include crossreferences.

Schwarz, David, Steve Ryan, and Fred Wostbrock. The Encyclopedia of TV Game Shows. 2nd ed. New York: Facts on File, 1995. 341p. il. show name, personal name, and profession indexes. $45.00. ISBN 0-8160-3093-6.
Arranged alphabetically by program, the text is both informative and highly readable. This edition also represents a significant upgrade over its predecessor, including over 100 shows which debuted between 1987-1995 and expanded cove rage in many of the original entries. Other strengths include an insightful 8,000-word introduction and appendixes listing programs that began on the radio or that have received awards.

Terrace, Vincent. Encyclopedia of Television: Series, Pilots, and Specials. 3 volumes. New York: New York Zoetrope, c1985-c1986. indexes.
The work lists over 7,000 series, pilots, specials, and experimental programs, arranged alphabetically by title. Volume 1 covers 1937-1973; volume 2, 1974-1984. Each entry provides genre classification, story line or content, cast production credits, network affiliation, show length, and dates program originally aired. Volume 3 is comprised of separate indexes for performers, producers, directors, and writers; credits cite entry numbers within the main text.

Waggett, Garard J. The Soap Opera Encyclopedia. New York: HarperCollins, 1997. 644p. il. $7.50 pap. ISBN 0061011576.

Covers nearly 100 soaps from the first half century of television. The entries, arranged alphabetically program title, include a historical survey of the show, star profiles, cast data, backstage anecdotes, annual ratings, and episode storylines. A feast for trivia buffs.

Individual Actors, Characters, and Programs

--Monty Python

Ross, Robert. The Monty Python Encyclopedia. TV Books Inc., 1999. 272 p. il. $22.00 pap. ISBN 1575000369.
An engaging compendium which delineates the characters, comic skits, and cultural impact of the landmark British program which first aired in the U.S. in 1970 on the Public Broadcasting System.

--Shatner, William (See also: *Star Trek*)

Schnakenberg, Robert E. The Encyclopedia Shatnerica. Renaissance, 1998. 256p. il. $14.95 pap. ISBN 1580630391.
The work provides factual material and critical assessments of all aspects of Shatner's professional career: the wide array of television credits (e.g., *Star Trek*, *T.J. Hooker*), film roles (e.g., *The Twilight Zone*, *Judgement at Nuremberg*), singing stints, and books authored (both science fiction and career reflections). Shatner's personal side is also explored at length, including a UFO experience and numerous testaments to his overweening vanity (e.g., demands that airbrushing be applied to render certain portions of his anatomy in a more pleasing light, heavy use of toupees and hair weaves).

--Star Trek

Howarth, Chris, with Steve Lyons. The Completely Useless Unauthorized Star Trek Encyclopedia. London Bridge, 1997. $5.95 trade pap. ISBN 0753501988.
A compilation of randomly assembled peripheral facts about *Star Trek*. The entries are arranged alphabetically by an intriguing array of headings (e.g., "Auto-Destruct," "The Love Boat" (romantic tension), "Yangs"). The narrative is humorous--often interjecting sarcasm and parody--in tone. The fact that the authors are British, and make repeated references to that nation's popular culture (e.g., TV 21), might represent a potential drawback for some readers.

Okuda, Michael, and Denise Okuda The Star Trek Encyclopedia: A Reference Guide to the Future. Doug Drexler, illustrator; Margaret Clark, photographer. New York: Pocket Books, 1997. 640p. il. $50.00. ISBN 0671536079.
This well researched volume continues to cover all information relating to the ever expanding Star Trek universe, including cast, story lines, alien races, solar systems, weapons, medical equipment, and "inside gags." The more than 2,000 illustrations and diagrams document starships, props, phasers, uniform emblems, various forms of technology. The 5,000-plus alphabetically arranged entries are complemented by extensive cross-referencing.

--X-Files

Hatfield, James, and George Burt. The Unauthorized X-Cyclopedia. Kensington Publishing Corporation, 1997. 336p. $15.00 pap. ISBN 1575662337.
Covers *X-Files* up through its fourth season. Utilizing an encyclopedic format (entries spanning Anasazi to Zirinka), the work provides information on all fictional characters, real- life actors, objects, and locations associated with the series. Also includes plot summaries and other data relating to each episode.

GUIDES TO THE LITERATURE--TELEVISION

Cassata, Mary, and Thomas Skill. Television: A Guide to the Literature. Phoenix, AZ: Oryx, 1985. 148p. author, title and subject indexes. ISBN 0-89774-140-4.
The work consists of three expanded bibliographic essays that originally appeared in *Choice* (Volume 19, 1982), on test patterns (overview of the field, historical development, reference sources); the environment (processes and effects of television, news, politics); and directions (the industry, criticism, collected works).

HANDBOOKS--FILM INDUSTRY

General

Adrian, Werner. Speed: The Cinema of Motion. New York: Bounty Books, 1975. 111p. $2.95 pap. ISBN 0-517-525763.
Motion in the movies comprises the theme of this slim volume which includes a center sectio n of color movie poster reproductions. All types of movies dealing with speed are included here such as aviation, racing, railroad, and biker films.

Annan, David. Ape: Monster of the Movies. New York: Bounty Books, 1975. 95p. il. $3.98. ISBN 0-517-521563.
This well- illustrated volume delves into the presence of simians in the movies, ranging from *King Kong* to *The Planet of the Apes* series. Films dealing with ape- like creatures are also included, such as *Return of the Ape Man*, *Bride of the Gorilla*, and *Dr. Renault's Secret*.

Annan, David. Robot: The Mechanical Monster. New York: Bounty Books, 1976. 111p. il. $4.95. ISBN 0-517-525984.
Mechanical men and women in films is the basis of this book which looks at movies which contain robots. Among them are the female robot in Metropolis in 1926 followed by an array of

such creatures, including Tobor the Great, Robby the Robot in *Forbidden Planet*, and The Colossus of New York. The book contains several color pages of movie poster reproductions.

Borst, Ronald V., with Keith Burns, Leith Adams, and Margaret A. Borst. Graven Images. New York: Grove Press, 1992. 240p. $50.00. ISBN 0-8201-1522-5.
A tremendous collection of poster and lobby card reproductions from horror, fantasy, and science fiction movies from the silent days into the 1960s. Almost everything is covered here, from classics like *Dracula* (1931) and *Frankenstein* (1931) to the very obscure, such as *The Horror* (1934). Stephen King wrote the introduction and those providing reminiscences include Robert Bloch, Clive Barker, Ray Bradbury, Harlan Ellison, and Peter Straub.

Hofstede, David. Hollywood Heroes. Lanham, MD: Madison Books, 1994. 282p. il. $22.95. ISBN 1-56833-029-4.
A variety of fictional characters and real life personalities identified as screen heroes are profiled in this entertaining volume. Each subject--including King Arthur, Batman, James Bond, Davy Crockett, Hercules, Bruce Lee, The Lone Ranger, Audie Murphy, Eliot Ness, Robin Hood, Rocky, Superman, Tarzan, Dick Tracy, and Zorro-- is allotted a chapter and a filmography.

London, Rose. Zombie: The Living Dead. New York: Bounty Books, 1976. 111p. $4.95. ISBN 0-517-525976.
Movies about the walking dead are discussed in this well written book which contains a bit more pictures than text. Still thorough coverage is given to such shockers as *White Zombie*, *I Walked With a Zombie*, *Dead Men Walk*, and *Voodoo Island*, plus various vampire, mummy and other horror thrillers.

Medved, Harry and Dreyfuss, Randy. The Fifty Worst Films of All Time. New York: Popular Library, 1978. 288p. $6.95 pap. ISBN 0-445-04139-0.
Two teenagers wrote this compilation claiming to discuss the fifty worst movies ever made. Among them they include D.W. Griffith's *Abraham Lincoln* (1930), Sergei Eisenstein's *Ivan the Terrible, Parts I & II* (1946-47), and Cecil B. DeMille's *Northwest Mounted Police* (1940). Not only do the authors show a decided lack of cinema history knowledge, they appear to also enjoy making fun of inoffensive programmers like

The Big Noise (1944) with Laurel and Hardy, *Daughter of The Jungle* (1949), *Jet Attack* (1958), and Gene Autry's *Twilight on the Rio Grande* (1948). While the authors occasionally hit the mark (*At Long Last Love* (1975), *Last Year at Marienbad* (1962), *Myra Breckinridge* (1970)), they are, for the most part, pompous toward their subjects and cinematically ignorant.

Medved, Harry and Medved, Michael. The Golden Turkey Awards. New York: Perigee Books, 1980. 223p. $6.95 pap. ISBN 0-399-50463-X.
Here is the volume which catapulted the late Edward D. Wood Jr. to fame, naming him the worst film director of all time. The book also looks at over 400 movies (although one is a complete hoax) and claims to dish up the all-time worst cinematic moments, as well as worst actress and actor of all time, and a compendium of awful movies. Ironically, the movies and people derided here are far better than this self- serving and rid iculous book, which, in itself, is one of the worst ever written.

Meyers, Richard. For One Week Only: The World of Exploitation Films. Piscataway, NJ: New Century Publishers, 1983. 270p. il. $12.95 pap. ISBN 0-8329-0142-3.
Fun coverage of low budget exploitation films from the 1960s up through the early 1980s. Individual films and genres are explored under the umbrella chapters of sex, drugs and rock 'n' roll, violence, and horror. The book is also filled with scores of interesting photos and poster reproductions.

Michael, Paul, ed. The American Movies Reference Book: The Sound Era. Englewood Cliffs, N.J.: Prentice-Hall, 1969. 629p. $29.95. ISBN 13-028134-4.
Aided by James Robert Parish, John Robert Cocchi, Ray Hagen, and Jack Edmund Nolan, all of whom served as editors, this large volume was one of the first important attempts to corral credits for stars and movies in the sound era for general consumption. Following an introduction which discusses various genres, the book lists the sound era films, including studio and release year, for hundreds of film players. The second major section gives cast and credits for an equal number of feature films. There are also filmographies for producers and directors and a section listing various awards, including the Academy Awards and the National Board of Review Awards. This work served as a primer for the popularity and plethora of film books that were to follow.

Minton, Lynn. Movie Guide for Puzzled Parents. New York: Delta, 1984. 368p. $12.95 pap. ISBN 0-385-29336-4. Here is a book which is aimed at parents who want to know what movies their children should watch and which ones should be avoided. Descriptions of over 1,500 films are provided, the emphasis being on movies of the 1960s and 1970s. A useful guide for the cinema of that time period.

Genre Studies

Adams, Les and Rainey, Buck. Shoot-Em-Ups. New Rochelle, NY: Arlington House, 1978. 633p. $35.00. ISBN 0-87000-393-3. A colossal work covering the Western movie from the silent era into the 1970s. Various chapters look at the transition of the cowboy movie from the earliest flickers to wide screen epics. The silent era is covered in the initial chapter and the rest are given over to sound films with cast and credits for some 3,339 titles. There is also a list of Continental Westerns, and an alphabetical listing of sound Westerns also serves as an index. The volume is succinctly written and profusely illustrated. A real must for any lover of the Western. The book was reprinted by Scarecrow Press in 1985 ($49.50; ISBN 0-8108-1848-5).

Barbour, Alan G. Days of Thrills and Adventure. New York: Macmillan, 1970. 168p. $3.95 pap. Basically a picture book with brief text, this volume covers the motion picture serial in the sound era. Included are independent cliffhangers, comic strip characters on film, heroes and heroines, masked villains, science fiction, and other topics related to the genre. The book's main asset is an array of photographs, but there is also a list of all sound serials by company listing the star, number of chapters, and release year.

Barbour, Alan G. Cliffhanger: A Pictorial History of the Motion Picture Serial. New York: A & W Publishers, 1977. 248p. il. $14.95. ISBN 0-89104-070-6. This handsome volume is short on text but long on pictures in telling the story of movie serials. Although this genre had its greatest popularity during the silent era only one brief chapter is given to this time period with the rest of the book illustrating sound cliffhangers. A listing of all sound serials by company is also included.

Barbour, Alan G. A Thousand and One Delights. New York: Macmillan, 1970. 177p. il. $3.95 pap.

With limited text, this pictorial volume covers mainly
1940s movies with a chapter on Maria Montez and Jon Hall,
followed by ones on Abbott and Costello, fantasy and horror
movies, comedies, Monogram Pictures, serial, detectives,
westerns, adventure films, and John Wayne. Basically a
pictorial, albeit, entertaining hodge-podge.

Barbour, Alan G. The Thrill of It All. New York:
Macmillan, 1970. 204p. il. $3.95 pap.
Still another pictorial volume from Alan G. Barbour, this
time dealing with western movies. This may be the most useful
of Barbour's picture books, not only for its illustrations
but for a more in-depth, and informative, text. After an opening
chapter on the silent comboys, the book covers the various
western heroes of the 1930s through the mid-1950s with special
emphasis on John Wayne, serials, trios, musical oaters,
villains, and serials. The last chapters covers the decline and
fall of the "B" western.

Baxter, John. Science Fiction in the Cinema. New York:
A.S. Barnes, 1970. 240p. il. $1.95 pap. ISBN 498-07416-X.
Early attempt to chronicle the history of the sci- fi cinema
with chapters on silent films, Things to Come, British
enteries, Jack Arnold's features, various monsters, and
futuristic cinema. The book is aided by readable text, interesting
photos, and a selected filmography.

Cocchi, John. Second Feature: The Best of the "B" Films.
Secaucus, NJ: Citadel Press, 1991. 256p. il. $16.95 pap. ISBN
0-8065-1186-9.
A variety of low budget movies from the 1930s to the 1950s
are thoughtfully discussed in this fun to read effort. Covered
by genres, the movies include comedies, dramas, westerns,
mysteries, crime, action, adventure, horror, fantasy, science
fiction, and musicals. As much fun as the text is, the inclusion
of dozens of photographs, including the reproductions of minor
studio logos, makes for an even better product.

Cross, Robin. The Big Book of B Movies, Or How Low
Was My Budget. New York: St. Martin's Press, 1981. 208p.
il. $10.95 pap. ISBN 0-312-07843-9.
Heavy on photos but short on text, this oversized softbound
book takes a condescending look at low budget movies from the
1930s into the 1960s. Various genres are covered including
thrillers, series films, serials, westerns, horror and sci- fi movies,
war pictures, musicals, comedies, costume dramas, epics,

and teenage dramas. There is also a picture gallery of genre stars.

Davies, David Stuart. Holmes of the Movies. New York: Bramhall House, 1976. 175p. $12.50. ISBN 0-517-232790. A concise and thorough study of Sherlock Holmes in the movies, with a foreword by Peter Cushing, who portrayed the sleuth in two films and on TV. One of the best books written about the cinema Holmes, it also contains a filmography.

Essoe, Gabe. Tarzan of the Movies. New York: Citadel Press, 1968. 208p. il. $8.95.
A thorough history of Tarzan on the screen from Elmo Lincoln through Ron Ely, is presented in this well written and finely illustrated volume. All the movies about the legendary character, including those of Johnny Weissmuller, Lex Barker, and Gordon Scott, are discussed and a bonus chapters includes imitations, satires, and ripoffs of Edgar Rice Burroughs' famous ape man.

Everman, Welch. Cult Horror Films. New York: Citadel Press, 1995. 229p. il. $17.95 pap. ISBN 0-8065-1425-6.
Dozens of low budget horror movie favorites are covered in this fun book, which is also nicely illustrated. While credit information is brief, a video source for each title is given and the movies are discussed in an informative and entertaining manner. Titles covered include *The Astro-Zombies, Blacula, Dementia 13, Freaks, The Giant Gila Monster, The Hideous Sun Demon, Lady Frankenstein, Lady Frankenstein, Mania, Phantom From Space, Space, Queen of Blood, Satan's Cheerleaders, The Terror, The Terror, The Toolbox Murders,* and *The Unearthly*.

Everman, Welch. Cult Science Fiction Films. New York: Citadel Press, 1995. 255p. il. $17.95 pap. ISBN 0-8065-1602-X.
Using the same format as the previous work, the author analyzes seventy- five sci- fi movies, ranging from big budget efforts like *The Boys From Brazil* to such schlock classics as *Frankenstein's Daughter*. Like the former volume, this one too is filled with neat pictures, and is fun to read.

Everson, William K. The Bad Guys. New York: Citadel Press, 1964. 241p. il. $6.95.

A loving tribute to the legion of movie villains who have
entertained moviegoers since the silent days is presented in
this handsome volume which contains score of pictures.
All types of bad guys, including master criminals, western
outlaws, gangsters, monsters, psychos, seducers, and spies are
included, as is a chapter on bad girls. Dedicated to Charles
King, and naming Noah Berry the badest bad guy them all, the
book includes such colorful villains as Lionel Atwill, Henry
Daniel, Sydney Greenstreet, Rudolph Klein-Rogge, Montagu
Love, Adolphe Menjou, J. Carrol Naish, Warner Oland, Paul
Panzer, Gustav von Seyffertitz, George Sanders, Erich
von Stroheim, Lawrence Tierney, and Tod Slaughter.

Everson, William K. Classics of the Horror Film.
Secaucus, NJ: Citadel Press, 1974. 246p. il. $12.00.
ISBN 0-8065-0437-4.
A well illustrated and lucid account of some three dozen
horror film classics such as *Frankenstein*, *Vampyr*, *Freaks*,
The Old Dark House, *Island of Lost Souls*, *Dracula*, *The Body
Snatcher*, *The Mummy*, *White Zombie*, *Cat People*, and *The
Phantom of the Opera*. Lesser known titles like *Murder By
the Clock*, *Murders in the Zoo*, *The Night Has Eyes*, and
Strangler of the Swamp are also covered. Also discussed are
vampire and werewolf chillers, Edgar Allan Poe films and old
house, hauntings, and possession features.

Everson, William K. The Detective in Film. Secaucus,
NJ: Citadel Press, 1972. 247p. il. $9.95. ISBN
0-8065-0298-3.
More of a pictorial history than an indepth study of the
detective film genre, this readable book traces the history
of the genre from silent films into the early 1970s with an
emphasis on a variety of subjects. These include Sherlock
Holmes, silent sleuths, early talkies, Oriental detectives,
British films, Alfred Hitchcock, and private eyes.

Everson, William K. A Pictorial History of the Western
Film. New York: Citadel Press, 1969. 246p. il. $10.00.
Containing more than 500 photographs, this volume covers
the history of the western cinema from *The Great Train Robbery*
into the late 1960s, when the genre was going into decline.
Equal time is given to the various stars of cowboy films and
the movies themselves, especially the grandiose westerns of
the 1950s and 1960s. The volume makes for fairly interesting
reading, but it is hardly a definitive study.

Eyles, Allen. The Western. New York: A.S. Barnes, 1975. 208p. il. film index. $8.95. ISBN 0-498-01323-5.
Covers the careers of over 400 persons associated with the western film with a brief look at their genre contributions. Includes a filmography.

Eyles, Allen, Robert Adkinson, and Nicholas Fry, editors. The House of Horror: The Story of Hammer Films. London: Lorrimer Publishing, 1973. 127p. il. ISBN 0-85647-020-1.
One of the first, and probably the best, studies of the British studio. Hammer Films majored in making horror pictures in the 1950s to the early 1970s. The book tells the history of the studio beginning in the mid-1930s while focusing on its greatest successes (e.g., the Frankenstein and Dracula series). Includes a thorough filmography.

Fenin, George N., and William K. Everson. The Western: From Silents to Cinerama. New York: Bonanza Books, 1962. 362p. il. $3.95.
Early attempt to present a history of the western movie from the days of the earliest flickers to the wide screen productions of the early 1960s. For the most part the authors do an admirable job in treading ground which was largely untilled at the time. The text is complemented by attractive illustrations.

Frank, Alan G. Horror Movies. London: Octopus Books, 1974. 160p. il.
Within a limited scope, this ambitious tome attempts to cover the history of the horror movie. It does so in a fairly good fashion, although the volumes' greatest asset is its fine array of photographs, some in color.
Frank, Alan G. Monsters and Vampires. London: Octopus Books, 1976. 160p. il. ISBN 7064-05250.
Like many Octopus titles, this book's best feature is its photographs. Here the author dissects the screen histories of such famous fright figures as vampires, Frankenstein's monster, mummies, Dr. Jekyll and Mr. Hyde, King Kong, Godzilla, and The Fly.

Gabree, John. Gangsters: From Little Caesar to the Godfather. New York: Pyramid Publications, 1973. 158p. il. $1.75 pap. ISBN 0-515-03249-2.
A concise and thoroughly enjoyable study of the gangster movie from the beginning of the sound era into the 1970s. Well illustrated, the book covers many genre classics like

Little Caesar, *The Public Enemy*, *High Sierra*, and *The Godfather* as well as many lesser known titles. A filmography is also provided.

Gifford, Denis. Movie Monsters. New York: Studio Vista/Dutton, 1969. 160p. il. $1.95 pap. ISBN 289-79701-2.
An early illustrated study of the horror film which looks at the genre from the perspective of various monsters, including Frankenstein, the Golem, the Mummy, and zombies, vampires, werewolves, etc. Lucid text and striking pictures.

Gifford, Denis. A Pictorial History of Horror Movies. London: Hamlyn, 1973. 216p. il. ISBN 0-600-36926-9.
The gamut of horror films from before the turn of the century into the 1970s are given laudable coverage in this handsomely illustrated book. The author looks at the films, their makers and the performers associated with the genre over the years. The text is highly enjoyable and informative and the photos well chosen.

Gifford, Denis. Science Fiction Film. New York: Studio Vista/Dutton, 1971. 160p. il. $2.95 pap. ISBN 289-1079-21.
A useful companion to Movie Monsters, this one discusses the science fiction film in terms of inventions (machines, rays, submarines), exploration, and future predictions. A top notch text and interesting pictures make for an entertaining work.

Glaessner, Verina. Kung Fu: The Cinema of Vengance. New York: Bounty Books, 1974. 134p. il. $2.95 pap. ISBN 0-517-518325.
Feature films, mostly Oriental, dealing with the art of Kung Fu are discussed in this heavily illustrated text. Although there is a brief look at the Yellow Peril films of the early cinema, most of the book is given over to movies of the 1960s and 1970s, highlighting such genre stars as Bruce Lee, Angela Mao, and Wang Yu. A center section reproduces color movie posters.

Glut, Donald F. Classic Movie Monsters. Metuchen, NJ: Scarecrow Press, 1978. 442p. il. $15.00. ISBN 0-8108-1049-2.
Nine of the most popular of movie monsters are thoroughly profiled in this book with coverage not only given to their films but also their appearances in other mediums, such as stage,

radio, television and literature. The monsters covered are The Wolf Man, Dr. Jekyll and Mr. Hyde, The Invisible Man, The Mummy, The Hunchback of Notre Dame, The Phantom of the Opera, The Creature From the Black Lagoon, King Kong, and Godzilla. Althoughly sparsely illustrated, the volume is a treasure trove of information on the monsters studied. In short, it is an important volume in the literature of the horror film.

Glut, Donald F. The Dracula Book. Metuchen, NJ: Scarecrow Press, 1975. 388p. $15.00. ISBN 0-81-08-0804-8. Bram Stoker's creation Count Dracula has been perhaps the most enduring of movie monsters and this volume presents a thorough study of the character as it has been presented in various mediums around the world. The main emphasis of the book is on motion pictures and movies about Dracula, from Nosferatu in 1922, through the 1931 Bela Lugosi's Dracula, and up to the mid-1970s when Christopher Lee was associated with the role. In fact, it is Lee's picture which is on the book's cover. This excellent work needs to be updated since Bela Lugosi, thanks to his cult following, is again considered the definitive Dracula.

Glut, Donald F. The Frankenstein Legend. Metuchen, NJ: Scarecrow Press, 1973. 320p. $10.00. ISBN 0-8108-0589-8. Almost every aspect of Mary Wollstonecraft Shelley's novel *Frankenstein* (1818) is covered in this book, from its early literary incarnations to the stage and Edison's first filming in 1910. The bulk of the book is given over to the various cinematic adaptations, the most famous being the 1931 Universal movie starring Boris Karloff as the monster. Every film which included the Frankenstein monster through the early 1970s is discussed in the volume as is the creature's radio and TV appearances. Literary pastiches and comic books are also covered. Like Glut's other works on movie monsters (see above), this one needs updating.

Grossman, Gary. Superman: Serial to Cereal. New York: Popular Library, 1976. 191p. il. $3.95 pap. A history of the Superman character in movies and TV, concentrating on the two Columbia serials starring Kirk Alyn, the 1940s cartoon series produced by Paramount and Fleischer Studios, and the 1950s television series starring George Reeves. The author not only writes lovingly of the character and its media offshoots, but he also includes many quotes from those directly involved with these productions. Loaded with interesting photographs, the book also contains a complete

list of the cartoons, a filmography for the serials, and a
cast list for each of the 104 TV programs. A treat for
Superman fans although it predates the theatrical films with
Christopher Reeve.

Haining, Peter. Agatha Christie: Murder in Four Acts.
London: Virgin, 1990. 160p. il. $22.95. ISBN 1-85227-273-2.
Entertainingly written, this volume provides thorough
coverage on the adaptations of Agatha Christie works on stage,
film, radio and television. In addition, her famed characters
Hercule Poirot, Miss Marple, and Tommy and Tuppence
Beresford are given individual chapters regarding their postliterary
careers. John Gielgud provides a brief introduction to
this nicely illustrated volume, which includes some color photos.

Haining, Peter. The Complete Maigret. London: Boxtree,
1994. 128p. il. $5.95 pap. ISBN 1-85283-447-1.
A thorough history of the films and TV shows based on
George Simenon's famous French sleuth Inspector Jules Maigret
is provided in this well researched volume. The character
has proved popular in many countries and all the international
actors to have portrayed Maigret are included, as is their
movies and small screen work. Includes a filmography.

Hanke, Ken. Charlie Chan at the Movies. Jefferson, NC:
McFarland, 1989. 286p. $42.50. ISBN 0-89950-427-2.
Laudable attempt to catalog information on all the Charlie
Chan movies starring Warner Oland, Sidney Toler, and Roland
Winters. Each of the forty-four features are analyzed in an
erudite manner with cast and credits included. Fans of the
Chan films will enjoy reading this volume almost as much as
watching the features.

Haydock, Ron. Deerstalker! Holmes and Watson on
Screen. Metuchen, NJ: Scarecrow Press, 1978. 326p.
$12.50. ISBN 0-8108-1061-1.
One of the best volumes compiled on the movies about Arthur
Conan Doyle's famed sle uth Sherlock Holmes and his associate,
Dr. John H. Watson. More than 400 Holmes movie and TV
appearances are chronicled in addition to discussing a variety of
Holmes-influenced counterparts, such as Sexton Blake and Craig
Kennedy. A must for all Sherlock Holmes film afficianados.

Hayes, David, and Brent Walker.. The Films of the Bowery.
Secaucus, NJ: Citadel Press, 1984. 224p. il. $19.95. ISBN
0-8065-0931-7.

Despite its title, this volume not only covers the Bowery Boys movies but also those of the Dead End Kids, Little Tough Guys and the East Side Kids. Cast, credits, plots, and analysis are given for each of the titles from 1937 to 1958. In addition, there are biographies of the players, principally Leo Gorcey, Huntz, Hall, Gabriel Dell, Billy Halop, Bobby Jordan, and Bernard Gorcey. Loaded with pictures, this volume is a fine tribute to these long lasting comedies.

Jones, Ken D., and Arthur F. McClure. Hollywood at War: The American Motion Picture and World War II. New York: A.S. Barnes & Co., 1973. 320p. il. $15.00. ISBN 0-498-01107-0.
Although it opens with an interesting essay about films in the period up to and including the Second World War, the vast bulk of this volume is simply a listing of cast and credits of war films, supplemented by dozens of photographs.

Kagan, Norman. The War Film. New York: Pyramid, 1974. 160p. il. $1.75 pap. ISBN 0-515-03483-5.
A concise look at Hollywood's involvement in war movies is provided in this readable text, the emphasis being on conflicts in this century. Only a handful of silent films (*Birth of a Nation*, *Wings*, *The Big Parade*) are covered in deference to many sound era outings, mostly on big budget productions. Well illustrated, the book provides a useful primer on Hollywood war movies.

Kinnard, Roy. The Blue and the Gray on the Silver Screen: More Than Eighty Years of Civil War Movies. Secaucus, NJ: Birch Lane Press, 1996. 284p. $24.95. ISBN 1-55972-383-1.
If one is looking for thorough coverage of Civil War films it will not be found in this volume. Several dozen feature films are included with credits, casts, and a perfunctory discussion, but only two of them are silent: D.W. Griffith's *Birth of a Nation* (1915) and *The General* (1927), starring Buster Keaton. Few titles are covered in depth and there is almost no historical perspective in discussing the various movies, which range from *Gone With the Wind* (1939) and *Friendly Persuasion* (!956) to *Mysterious Island* (1961), and *The Good, The Bad and the Ugly* (1967). An appendix claims to list Civil War movies from 1903 to 1929, but stops at 1921.

Kinnard, Roy. Fifty Years of Movie Serials. Metuchen, NJ: Scarecrow Press, 1983. 210p. ISBN 0-8108-1644-X.

A slender volume which provides a cursory look at motion picture serials with the emphasis on sound cliffhangers. Only two pages of text and an index is given for silent chapter plays, while short individual chapters and filmographies are provided for the sound serials of Mascot, Republic, Columbia, Universal, and various independents. Interviews with Buster Crabbe and Jean Rogers are also included.

Kobal, John. Gotta Sing Gotta Dance: A Pictorial History of Film Musicals. London: Hamlyn, 1971. 320p. il. ISBN 0-600-03126-8.
Superb accounting of the movie musical filled with dozens of well chosen photographs. Covered are the early sound musicals, the classics of the 1930s, and the golden age of the 1940s, plus the big budget outings of the 1950s and 1960s. A very interesting chapter deals with the foreign film musical, particularly those from Great Britain.

Lahue, Kalton C. Bound and Bagged: The Story of the Silent Serials. New York: A.S. Barnes, 1968. 352p. $7.50. il. ISBN 68-14412.
Serials were one of the most popular genres in the silent days, especially in the teens, and this volume traces the history of the genre with emphasis on stars (Pearl White, Ruth Roland, Eddie Polo, William Desmond, Helen Holmes, etc.) and outrageous plots. The operations of the noted serial factories, such as Pathe, Universal, Mascot, Vitagraph, and Rayart, are also outlined. Filled with interesting pictures, the volume also includes the script for the first episode of the 1920 Pathe cliffhanger *Pirate Gold*.

Lahue, Kalton C. World of Laughter: The Motion Picture Comedy Short, 1910-1930. Norman, OK: University of Oklahoma Press, 1966. 240p. $4.95.
The history of American film comedy in the silent era is recounted in this readable volume. The various companies (Keystone, Universal, etc.) are covered as are the myraid of stars like John Bunny, Fatty Arbuckle, Wallace Berry, Ben Turpin, Charlie Chaplin, Billy West, Ford Sterling, The Keystone Kops, Charley Chase, Al St. John, Billy Bevan, Harry Langdon, Mabel Normand, Larry Semon, Harold Lloyd, and Dot Farley. An appendix listing the releases of various noted comedians is also included.

Lentz, Harris M. III. Science Fiction, Horror & Fantasy Film and Televison Credits. Jefferson, NC: McFarland, 1983. 1374p. (2 vol.). $69.95. ISBN 0-89950-071-4.

The work provides genre filmographies for hundreds of performers and also includes TV credits. When known, the character name played by the actor or actress is also provided. The first volume also includes the same information for various producers, directors, writers, and other film technicians. Volume two gives the director and casts for genre films and TV shows. A third volume, *Science Fiction, Horror & Fantasy Film and Television Credits; Supplement I: Through 1987* (Jefferson, NC: McFarland, 1989. 936p. $89.00. ISBN 0-89950-364-0), by the same author complements the set.

Maltin, Leonard. The Great Movie Shorts. New York: Crown Publishers, 1972. 236p. $9.95.
Thorough coverage of the motion picture short subject field from the 1930s into the 1950s. Profiles output from various studios like Hal Roach, Columbia, RKO, Educational, Paramount, and Warners as well as numerous series such as *Our Gang*, *Pete Smith Specialties*, *Screen Snapshots*, and *Voice of Hollywood*, and stars like Laurel and Hardy, Charley Chase, Harry Langdon, Buster Keaton, Edgar Kennedy, Leon Errol, and Clark & McCullough. Newsreels, travelogues, documentaries, musicals, and sports films are also denoted in this well done compilation.

Miller, Don. Hollywood Corral. New York: Popular Library, 1976. 255p. il. $3.95 pap. ISBN 445-08443-395.
Probably the best book ever written on the low budget western film, this volume is equally good for its lucid text and memorable photographs, most of which came from the Jan Barfode collection. Author Don Miller delved into his immense knowledge of motion picture history to give vivid coverage to the genre of the "B" western from the beginning of the sound era (there is a short chapters on silent oaters) to its demise in the mid-1950s. The text is mainly geared to genre stars and all of them, big and small, are included with special emphasis on Hoot Gibson, Ken Maynard, Tom Mix, Buck Jones, Tim McCoy, Bob Steele, Tom Tyler, John Wayne, George O'Brien, Tim Holt, Tom Keene, Gene Autry, Roy Rogers, Charles Starrett, The Three Mesquiteers, The Range Busters, Bill Elliott, and Johnny Mack Brown. A volume to be treasured by lovers of the cowboy stars of yore and their movies.

Muller, Eddie, and Daniel Faris. Grindhouse: The Forbidden World of "Adults Only" Cinema. New York: St. Martin's/ Griffin, 1996. 157p. $19.95 pap. ISBN 0-312-14609-4.

Fascinating coverage of the making of adult-oriented theatrical
movies from the 1920s into the 1970s complemented by an
abundance of illustrations. Individual films are discussed as
are the careers of producers such as Dwain Esper, Kroger Babb,
George Weiss, Doris Wishman, Russ Mayer, and David Friedman.
An informative and enjoyable look at a genre long gone from the
entertainment scene.

Nance, Scott. Bloodsuckers: Vampires at the Movies. Las
Vegas, Nevada: Pioneers Books, 1992. 149p. il. $14.95 pap.
ISBN 1-55698-317-4.
Perfunctory look at the history of the vampire film
with light discussion of many titles sprinkled with some
illustrations. An appendix lists hundreds of titles, both
foreign and domestic, with release year, country, and stars.
Not an in-depth work.

Ottoson, Robert. A Reference Guide to the American
Film Noir: 1940-1958. Metuchen, NJ: Scarecrow Press,
1981. 290p. il. $15.00. ISBN 0-8108-1363-7.
Hollywood films dealing with the "dark cinema" of the
1940s and 1950s are studied in this book which takes a brief
look at over 250 of these titles. Providing concise cast and
credits for each movie, the author discusses the films in a
few paragraphs each but the text is informative and entertaining.
While the emphasis is on "A" studio productions, low budget
affairs like *Detour* (1945) and *So Dark the Night* (1946) also
get their due. A useful bibliography is also provided.

Palmer, Scott. The Films of Agatha Christie. London:
B.T. Batsford, 1993. 226p. il. $25. ISBN 0-7134-7205-7.
All of the feature films and TV movies based on the works
of Agatha Christie are given thorough coverage in this volume,
which is filled with stills from the various productions. Each
movie is discussed in detail with a complete cast list. TV
shows are given a bit less coverage, but the book overall is a
fine compendium of the screen adaptations of Christie's books
and short stories.

Parish, James Robert, and George H. Hill. Black Action.
Jefferson, NC: McFarland, 1989. 399p. $55.00. ISBN
0-89950-456-6.
A lengthy filmography discussing dozens of black oriented
action movies, mainly from the 1970s and 1980s. For each
film, complete cast and credits are provided, as is a plot
synopsis and critical analysis. An interesting volume on

an intriguing cinema genre which appears to have faded in
the 1990s.

Parish, James Robert. The Great Combat Pictures.
Metuchen, NJ: Scarecrow Press, 1990. 486p. $52.00. ISBN
0-8108-2315-2.
A look at twentieth century warfare as portrayed on the
silver screen is presented in this detailed volume which includes
a plethora of feature films involved all U.S. wars since 1917.
Each film is discussed along with cast, credits, and plots.
A useful look at the subject of how military engagements have
been transferred to the movies.

Parish, James Robert. The Great Cop Pictures.
Metuchen, NJ: Scarecrow Press, 1990. 693p. il. $62.50.
ISBN 0-8108-2316-0.
More than 330 U.S. feature films and TV movies covering
the period from the 1920s into the 1980s are analyzed in this
source. The police action film has always been a staple
money maker for Hollywood and the book delves into the
reason for this in covering a variety of police pictures. For
each title there is cast and credits, plot synopsis, and a
critical discussion of the film. Provides in-depth coverage
of this movie genre.

Parish, James Robert. The Great Movie Series. South
Brunswick, NJ: A.S. Barnes, 1971. 333p. il. $15.00. ISBN
0-498-07847-7.
One of the first volumes to come out at the beginning of
the onrush of cinema literature in the late 1960s and early
1970s, this work covers twenty-five Hollywood movie
series, discussing each by title and providing filmographies.
Each series also is illustrated from stills from individual
films. The series covered are Andy Hardy, Blondie, Bomba,
Boston Blackie, Bowery Boys, Charlie Chan, Crime Doctor, Dr.
Christian, Dr. Kildare, Ellery Queen, The Falcon, Francis the
Talking Mule, Hopalong Cassidy, James Bond, Jungle Jim, The
Lone Wolf, Ma and Pa Kettle, Maisie, Matt Helm, Mr. Moto,
Philo Vance, The Saint, Sherlock Holmes, Tarzan, and The Thin
Man.

Parish, James Robert. Prison Pictures from Hollywood.
Jefferson, NC: McFarland, 1991. 544p. il. $62.50. ISBN
0-89950-563-5.
Enhanced by 85 photographs, this book discusses nearly 300
movies about prison life, including some made for television.

Each title includes cast, credits, plots, and critiques. It discusses an interesting variety of subjects, including *I Am a Fugitive From a Chain Gang* (1932), *Caged* (1950), and *Chained Heat* (1983).

Parkinson, Michael, and Clyde Jeavons. A Pictorial History of Westerns. London: Hamlyn, 1972. 217p. il. ISBN 0-600-13067-3.
Provides fairly thorough coverage of the western film genre. The authors discuss not only individual movies but also stars, character actors, directors, European oaters, and TV westerns. A healthy number of the photos are in color.

Pate, Janet. The Book of Sleuths. Chicago: Contemporary Books, 1977. 124p. $5.95 pap. ISBN 0-8092-7837-5.
Within limited space, the author concisely and thoroughly writes about the careers of dozens of fictional detectives and lists their appearances in other mediums, such as stage, film, radio and television. Among the slueths studied are C. Auguste Dupin, Sexton Blake, Sherlock Holmes, Hercule Poirot, Charlie Chan, Miss Marpe, The Saint, Dick Tracy, Inspector Maigret, The Toff, Philip Marlowe, Mike Hammer, John Shaft, and Kojak.

Pattison, Barrie. The Seal of Dracula. New York: Bounty Books, 1975. 136p. il. $2.95 pap. ISBN 0-517-521539.
One of the best books ever written about the vampire cinema, this heavily illustrated work, which includes a color section, discusses vampire movies from the silent days to the present. The volume looks at hundreds of feature films about film's most popular monster, ranging from the silent *Nosferatu* to the interpretations of Bela Lugosi and Christopher Lee. Many foreign films, including those of director Jean Rollin and Jess Franco, are also discussed. The book closes with a filmography.

Peary, Danny. Cult Movies. New York: Delta, 1981. 402p. il. $13.94 pap. ISBN 0-440-51647-1.
One hundred of "The Classics, the Sleepers, the Weird, and the Wonderful" movies are covered in this volume, which includes such titles as *All About Eve, Caged Head, Emmanuelle, Freaks, Gun Crazy, I Walked With a Zombie, Laura, Pink Flamingos, Rio Bravo, The Scarlet Empress, Targets,* and *The Wizard of Oz.* Overall the author's appraisals are interesting although one cannot help but wonder when he claims *Plan 9 From Outer Space* camouflaged anti-military sentiments.

Peary, Danny. Cult Movies 2. New York: Dell, 1983. 182p.
il. $12.95 pap. ISBN 0-440-51632-3.
An anemic follow-up to the previous volume, this one covers
only fifty cult films and the crop is not an especially interesting
one. Included are such film fare as *Barbarella*, *Blood Feast*,
Dark Star, *The First Nudie Musical*, *High School Confidential*,
Last Tango in Paris, *Phantom of Paradise*, *Taxi Driver*, and
Willy Wonka and the Chocolate Factory.

Pirie, David. A Heritage of Horror: The English Gothic
Cinema 1946-1972. New York: Avon, 1973. 192p. il. $2.95
pap. ISBN 0-380-00069-5.
An important document on the British gothic cinema, this
work discusses how the erotic and shock were combined to make
a unique cinema presence. Special emphasis is given to the
output of Hammer Films and its directors, Terence Fisher and
Freddie Frances, and writer James Sangster. Nicely illustrated,
the book also includes a filmography.

Pirie, David. The Vampire Cinema. New York: Crescent
Books, 1977. 176p. il. ISBN 0-517-20591-2.
Vampire movies are given their due in this profusely
illustrated volume, devoed to the legends of Vlad the Impaler
and Countess Elizabeth Bathory before actually delving into
such cinema fare as *Nosferatu*, Bela Lugosi's *Dracula* and
hundreds of other vampire films. The text is succinct and
the photos, some in color, nicely around out the work.

Rainey, Buck. The Reel Cowboy: Essays on the Myth in
Movies and Literature. Jefferson, NC: McFarland, 1996.
319p. $39.95. ISBN 0-7864-0106-0.
Here is a comparison between the real West and its cinema counterpart.
The author opens with an essay on how western films deserted realism
for box office. This is followed by a look at a number of western writers
and how their works were adapted to the screen. Major coverage is
given to Zane Grey, James Oliver Curwood, Jack London, and Rex
Beach. Also included are such scribes as Bertha M. Bower, Max
Brand, Walt Coburn, James Fennimore Cooper, Laurie York Erskine,
Hamlin Garland, Frank Gruber, Bret Harte, Ernest Haycox, Emerson
Hough, Peter B. Kyne, Louis L'Amour, William Colt MacDonald,
Clarence E. Mulford, Luke Short, Frank Hamilton Spearman, and
Harold Bell Wright. All the films based on a writer's work, including
cast and credits, are also given.

Searles. Baird. Films of Science Fiction and Fantasy. New York:
Harry N. Abrams, 1988. 240p. il. ISBN 0-8109-0922-7.

A large, attractive, heavily illustrated look at various science fiction and fantasy films, including space movies, time travel, dinosaurs and aliens. A fairly interesting study with a perfunctory filmography.

Senn, Bryan. Golden Horrors: An Illustrated Critical Filmography, 1931-1939. Jefferson, NC: McFarland, 1996. 528p. $55.00. ISBN 0-7864-0175-3.
A thoroughly enjoyable tome which covers most of the Popular horror films of the 1930s, ranging from well known Titles like *King Kong* (1933) and *Son of Frankenstein* (1939) to obscure items such as *The Secret of the Loch* (1934) and *Torture Ship* (1939). The author provides detailed information and useful insights into each of the movies in the context of a very readable text. In addition to the coverage given the major movies, there is also an appendix with less information on titles that have peripheral horror elements. An extremely useful addition to literature on the horror film.

Sherman, Samuel M. Legendary Singing Cowboys. New York: Friedman/Fairfax, 1995. 64p. il. ISBN 1-56799-229-5.
Brief but highly informative study of the singing cowboy and the westerns they made from the 1930s through the 1950s. Covers such stars are Gene Autry, Roy Rogers, Eddie Dean, Dick Foran, Ray Whitley, The Sons of the Pioneers, Tex Ritter, Herb Jeffries, Jimmy Wakely, Rex Allen, and many others. Packaged with a compact disc which contains songs recorded by some of the stars profiled in the book.

Springer, John. All Talking! All Singing! All Dancing! New York: Citadel Press, 1966. 256p. il. $5.95.
The first, and one of the best, studies of the movie musical, this pictorial history covers the genre from the late 1920s through the mid-1960s in hundreds of photographs and succinct text. Lists of memorable movie songs are also included. A fun and informative volume, the text does contain a few errors (i.e., Nick Lucas' surname is spelled Lukas), but it remains a delightful primer on its subject. Reissued by Cadillac Books in the 1970s.

Steinbrunner, Chris, and Burt Goldbatt. Cinema of the Fantastic. New York: Galahad Books, 1972. 282p. il. $12.50. ISBN 0-88365-256-0.
Lengthy essays and illustrations on fifteen ground breaking fanstasy movies make up this volume. The films covered are *A Trip to the Moon, Metropolis, Freaks, King Kong, The Black Cat, The Bride of Frankenstein, Mad Love, Flash Gordon,*

Things to Come, The Thief of Bagdad, Beauty and the Beast, The Thing, 20,000 Leagues Under the Sea, Invasion of the Body Snatchers (1956), and *Forbidden Planet.*

Steinbrunner, Chris, and Norman Michaels. The Films of Sherlock Holmes. Secaucus, NJ: Citadel Press, 1978. 253p. il. $14.95. ISBN 0-8065-0599-0.
Supplemented with lots of pictures, this volume covers the screen career of fiction's most famous sleuth, Sherlock Holmes. Beginning with the first Holmes movie in 1900, the book deals with such actors as John Barrymore, Clive Brook, Eille Norwood, and Reginald Owen in the part although the bulk of the coverage goes to Basil Rathbone's Holmes portrayals. Later Holmes movies are also studied, including Peter Cushing's *The Hound of the Baskervilles.* There is also a chapter on Holmes and television.

Stern, Lee Edward. The Movie Musical. New York: Pyramid, 1974. 160p. il. $1.75 pap. ISBN 0-515-03487-7.
This entry in the Pyramid Illustrated History of the Movies series reads like a lengthy magazine piece but is informative and entertaining. Musical films from the dawn of sound releases to the early 1970s are studied in a concise, albeit knowing, manner. Includes a filmography.

Sternfield, Jonathan. The Look of Horror: Scary Moments from Scary Movies. New York: M & M Books, 1990. 144p. il. ISBN 0-89471-831-2.
This oversized volume takes a cursory look at 70 scary movies dealing with monsters, aliens, murderers, maniacs, mad doctors, creatures, bad and weird kids, ghosts and demons, etc. Only for the uninitiated.

Strick, Philip. Science Fiction Movies. London: Octopus Books, 1976. 160p. ISBN 0-7064-0470X.
A plethora of sci- fi movies are looked at in this heavily illustrated volume with the pictures being the book's best attribute. The author discusses movies in the context of subjects like invading aliens, mad scientists, monsters, and time travel.

Svehla, Gary J., and Susan Svehla, editors. Guilty Pleasures of the Horror Film. Baltimore, MD: Midnight Marquee Press, 1996. 256p. $20.00 pap. ISBN 1-887664-03-3.
A delightful series of essays on various writers' favorite worst film. Among the chosen are *Maniac, Sh! The Octopus, Voodoo*

Man, Two Lost Worlds, The Indestructible Man, Rodan, The Tingler, When Dinosaurs Ruled the Earth, the 1976 version Of *King Kong*, and *Dune*. The various scribes make pretty Good cases for their selections, and each title includes cast and credits. Some of the titles here are more fun to read about than watch.

Tohill, Cathal, and Tombs, Pete. Immoral Tales: European Sex and Horror Movies 1956-1984. New York: St. Martin's/ Griffin, 1994. 272p. il. $17.95 pap. ISBN 0-312-13519-X. The authors of this oversized softbound tome have done a fine job in discussing the European sex and horror movies from the mid-1950s to the mid-1980s. Not only do they cover films from Italy, Germany, France, and Spain, but the careers of such directors as Jess Franco, Jean Rollin, Jose Larraz, Walerian Borowczyk, and Alain Robbe-Grillet are also discussed in a literate manner. There is also an appendix with biographies of crafts people and performers associated with these movies, plus a section on adult comic books. While nicely illustrated, including a color section, the book contains some sexually graphic photos.

Tombs, Pete. Mondo Macabro: Weird & Wonderful Cinema Around the World. New York: St. Martin's/Griffin, 1997. 192p. il. $18.95 pap. ISBN 0-312-18748-3. Having co-authored a similar volume, *Immoral Tales* (q.v.), Pete Tombs tackles ho rror and sex films from such diverse places as Hong Kong, the Philippines, Indonesia, India, Turkey, Brazil, Argentina, Mexico and Japan. A literate and well-researched text is supplemented by a horde of photos, some in color and some sexually explicit, fo r a look at a side of the cinema little covered in other books. Drawbacks include very small print and a poorly conceived index.

Turner, George E. and Price, Michael H. Forgotten Horrors: Early Talkie Chillers from Poverty Row. Cranbury, NJ: A.S. Barnes, 1979. 216p. $19.95. il. ISBN 0-498-02136-X. One of the finest film books ever written, this volume zeroes in on obscure horror, adventure and mystery movies which came from Hollywood's Poverty Row in the 1929-37 period. Cast, credits, plots, and analysis is provided for each title along with many interesting photographs. The book is as entertaining as its subject, and is filled with a mass of information done is a very readable style. A slightly revised edition was published by Eclipse Books in 1986.

Van Hise, James. Calling, Tracy!: Six Decades of Dick Tracy. Las Vegas, NV: Pioneer Books, 1990. 148p. il. $14.95 pap. ISBN 1-55698-241-0.
While this volume provides a potpourri of information on Chester Gould's famous comic strip character Dick Tracy, the bulk of the book is given over to the serials and feature films about the detective. Also included is a history of the strip, Tracy on radio and TV, and collectibles.

Warren, Bill. Keep Watching the Skies! Jefferson, NC: McFarland, 1982. 467p. $39.95. ISBN 0-89950-032-3.
A landmark volume in the area of science fiction films. The author deftly discusses all U.S. released sci- fi movies for the years 1950 through 1957. He not only provides the plots and background on the films, but also useful insights which will delight the reader. Cast and credits for each title are also provided, as is a list of motion picture serials for the years covered.

Warren, Bill. Keep Watching the Skies! Volume II. Jefferson, NC: McFarland, 1986. 839p. $69.95. ISBN 0-89950-170-2.
The author's equally fine follow-up to the above volume, this one giving coverage to sci- fi movies in the 1958-1962 period. Since more genre movies came out during that time period, the second volume is twice as large as the first. Again cast and credits are provided as well as an addenda to the first volume. Taken together, these two books provide the best coverage for science fiction movies for the years 1950 through 1962. In 1998, the two books were combined into a single softbound volume, *Keep Watching the Skies! American Science Fiction Movies of the Fifties* (Jefferson, NC: McFarland Classics, 1998. 1344p. $35 pap. ISBN 0-786-40479-5).

Weisser, Thomas. Spaghetti Westerns - The Good, The Bad and the Violent: 558 Eurowesterns and Their Personnel, 1961-1977. Jefferson, NC: McFarland, 1989. 498p. $49.95. ISBN 0-89950-688-7.
An excellent reference source on the genre of the European western, which was in vogue in the late 1960s and early 1970s. The author covers hundreds of these films giving original and English titles, casts and credits, plot synopsis, and brief critical analysis. While the comments on the films are not involved, the text is very informative. The book is also spiced with many stills and poster reproductions. Useful appendices

for performers, directors, scriptwriters, music composers, and cinematographers are also included. This volume is one of McFarland's best reference works.

Worth, D. Earl. Sleaze Creatures. Key West, FL: Fantasma Books, 1995. 256p. il. $19.95 pap. ISBN 0-9634982-6-6.
Subtitled "An Illustrated Guide to Obscure Hollywood Horror Movies 1956-1959" this softbound provides fun reading about 50 low budget features, including *Bride of the Monter*, *The Indestructible Man*, *The She Creature*, *Blood of Dracula*, *The Astounding She Monster*, *Giant From The Unknown*, *Attack of the 50 Foot Woman*, *Earth vs. the Spider*, *Beast From Haunted Cave*, and *Terror is a Man*. Cast, credits and stills are provided for each title covered.

Historical and Sociological Studies

Anger, Kenneth. Hollywood Babylon. San Francisco: Straight Arrow Books, 1975. 307p.
A trashy pictorial look at film capitol scandals through the years covering many sensational stories such as the murders of William Desmond Taylor and Ramon Novarro and the love lives of Hollywood royalty. Followed by the equally sordid sequel Hollywood Babylon 2.

Behlmer, Rudy, and Thomas, Tony. Hollywood's Hollywood: The Movies About The Movies. Secaucus, NJ: The Citadel Press, 1975. $19.95. ISBN 0-8065-0491-9.
Hollywood's biggest love affair has always been with itself, as this ample volume proves. More than 200 movies, from the movies' earliest days into the mid-1970s, are covered with a plethora of still photographs. Although there are a number of omissions, the volume covers its subject in nice detail.

Brownlow, Kevin. The Parade's Gone By. New York: Alfred A. Knopf, 1968. 593p.
One of the most important books ever written on the silent picture in particular, and motion pictures in general. Through text and the personal recollections of many silent film personalities, the book covers aspects of early movie making, in addition to famous films, directors, and stars. The author's knowledge of the silent cinema is very evident in the text, which is enriched by the remembrances of those interviewed. A rich array of photographs also enchance the volume, one which should be read by every true film buff.

Brownlow, Kevin. The War, the West, and The
Wilderness. New York: Alfred A. Knpof, 1979. 602p.
$27.50. ISBN 0-394-48921-7.
A followup to the above work, this volume is another
must read tor true film lovers. This time the author looks at
silent films and a few early talkies in the context of World
War I, the West, and the wilderness. The book is a treasure
trove of cinema history, including first person accounts, and
the discussion of noted films, personalities, and themes. Like
its predecessor, a truly magnificent work.

Dixon, Wheeler. Producers Releasing Corporation: A
Comprehensive Filmography and History. Jefferson, NC:
McFarland, 1986. 166p. $19.95. ISBN 0-89950-179-6.
Despite its title this is a puny effort in presenting the
history of the 1940s poverty row studio Producers Releasing
Corporation (PRC). Among its chapters are a brief history
of the studio, short biographies of key personnel, an
interview with director Edgar G. Ulmer by Peter Bogdanovich,
and a checklist of the studio's releases.

Dooley, Roger. From Scarface to Scarlett: American
Films in the 1930s. New York: Harcourt Brace Janovich,
1981. 648p. $14.95 pap. ISBN 0-15-633998-6.
More than five thousand feature films, along with some
200 stills, are profiled in this well written and quite entertaining
volume. The author covers the various popular genres of the
period, such as gangsters, horror movies, westerns, crazy
comedies and spy thrillers, in addition to the big blockbusters
which culminated at the end of the decade with *Gone With the
Wind*. Although it mainly sticks to the "A" productions and
movies from the major studios, this book is well worth reading
and one of the best volumes to deal with the films of the 1930s.

Eames, John Douglas. The Paramount Story. New York:
Crown, 1985. 368p. $35.00. ISBN 0-517-55348-1.
This oversized volume discusses all the film releases of Paramount
Pictures from 1916 to 1984, with an emphasis on the sound era.
Its best asset is its numerous photographs, while the text makes for
interesting reading but only a peripheral reference tool.

Fernett, Gene. Poverty Row. Satellite Beach, FL: Coral
Coral Reef Publications, 1971. 163p. $10.00. ISBN
0-914042-02-7.
A look at the world of low budget Hollywood filmmakers is
presented by this illustrated book which mainly covers the

years 1930 to 1950. A number of studios (Tiffany, Monogram, Grand National, Republic, PRC) are profiled, as are several producers like the Weiss Brothers, Sam Katzman, C.C Burr, A.W. Hackel, Maurice Conn, and Robert L. Lippert. This volume casts only a perfunctory look at Poverty Row, and while more reliable than some of the author's books, it is basically a shallow effort.

Franklin, Joe. Classics of the Silent Screen. New York: Citadel Press, 1959. 254p. $6.95.
With the aid of research assistant William K. Everson, radio and TV variety show host Joe Franklin compiled this book, one of the earliest, and best, tributes to the silent screen. The volume contains two sections. The first discusses fifty great silent movies from *The Great Train Robbery* in 1903 to 1931's *Tabu*. The second section provides biographies of 75 silent films stars.

Giroux, Robert. A Dead of Death. New York: Alfred A. Knopf, 1990. 277p. $19.95. ISBN 0-394-58075-3.
A meticulously researched look into the still officially unsolved 1921 William Desmond Taylor murder case. The author reviews the facts in the case and says who killed Taylor, although he states the actual name of the person may never be known at this late date. The author makes a good case for his opinions, unlike the fanciful *A Cast Of Killers* (q.v.) which deals with the same subject. This book should be read by anyone interested in the Taylor case.

Griffith, Richard, and Arthur Mayer. The Movies. New York: Bonanza Books, 1957. 442p.
The history of the movies is detailed in this oversized volume which contains over 1,000 photographs. A primer for those beginning movie research, this well written and very informative volume covers a myraid in its entertaining look at the movies from the earliest flickers into the mid-1950s.

Jewell, Richard B., with Vernon Harbin. The RKO Story. New York: Arlington House, 1982. 320p. $35.00. ISBN 0-517-546566.
Coverage of every RKO (at times called Radio and RKO Radio) movies from 1929 to 1960 is provided in this handsomely illustrated oversized volume. The writeups

for each title, although brief, include cast, some credits, plot synopsis, and critical evaulation. In addition, there are sections on RKO British films, nominations and awards, and thorough indexes for tiles and personnel. A very well done and useful reference volume.

Kirkpatrick, Sidney D. A Company of Killers. New York: E.P. Dutton, 1986. 301p. $17.95. ISBN 0-525-24390-9.
Supposed study of the William Desmond Taylor murder case reads like a film scenario and is not to be taken seriously. Allegedly based on director King Vidor's research into the still unsolved homicide in 1922, the book claims to reveal the killer but it contains many so errors it is hard to take the work as little more than historical fiction.

Kisch, John, and Mapp, Edward. A Separate Cinema: Fifty Years of Black Cast Posters. New York: Noonday Press, 1992. 168p. $20.00 pap. ISBN 0-374-52360-6.
Filled with poster reproductions, mostly in color, from black cast movies from the silent days through the 1960, this volume is a monumental work in the area of black cinema history. With a preface by Spike Lee and an introduction by Donald Bogle, the volume reproduces dozens of posters from the past, including the work of such directors as Oscar Michaeaux and Spencer Williams, the films of Paul Robeson, Herb Jeffrey's cowboy movies, and the many musicals and comedies produced for the Negro film market from the 1920s through the 1940s. Concise text is included, giving an overall history of the Black cinema as it progressed from silent movies into the Civil Rights era.

Lahue, Kalton C., and Brewer, Terry. Kops and Custards: The Legend of Keystone Films. Norman, OK: University of Oklahoma Press, 1968. 177p. $4.95.
Mack Sennett's Keystone Film Company is highlighted in this well researched book which provides information on not only hundreds of comedies, but also many of the studio's stars, such as Ford Sterling, Mabel Normand, Fatty Arbuckle, Charlie Chaplin, Ben Turpin, Charley Murray, and the Sennett Bathing Beauties. All Keystone comedies released between 1912 and 1917 are listed in the book's filmography.

Lee, Raymond. Fit for the Chase. South Brunswick, NJ: A.S. Barnes, 1969. 237p. il. $8.50.

Photo volume tracing the history of the Tin Lizzie on film from the early silent days to the present. Showing how the auto has been used over the years in various guises as a movie prop, the author illustrates the evolution of the car as presented on screen.

Lee, Raymond. Not So Dumb: Animals in the Movies. South Brunswick, NJ: A.S. Barnes, 1970. 380p. il. $8.50. ISBN 498-07525-7.
A pictorial survey with vignettes about many of the famous animals of the movies, this volume is a colorful look at its subject. Dog stars like Rin-Tin-Tin, Lassie, and Strongheart are discussed as are such horse heroes as Tony, Silver, Tarzan, Champion, Rex and Trigger. Cat stars like Rhubarb and Pepper are also included along with the chimp Cheetah and lion stars Numa and Duke. A fun excursion into the wildlife of the movies.

Lee, Ray(mond). A Pictorial History of Hollywood Nudity. Chicago: Merit Books, 1964. 128p. il. $0.75 pap.
Heavily illustrated but slender in text, this paperback traces the history of nudity in the movies from the silent days to just before the collapse of the production code in the 1960s. The volume is a fairly useful one in its look at such films as *Intolerance*, *Trader Horn*, the silent *Ben Hur*, *Dante's Inferno*, and *War of the Buttons*. Also included are such stars as Marlene Dietrich, Jayne Mansfield, Elke Sommer, Ramon Novarro, Marilyn Monroe, and Jean Harlow.

Leish, Kenneth W. Cinema. New York: Newsweek Books, 1974. 192p. il. ISBN 0-88225-109-0.
With over 200 illustrations, some in color, this volume studies the history of the movies from the days of D.W. Griffith and Mack Sennett, into the 1970s. While pictures dominate the work, the text is useful and often interesting.

Limbacher, James. Sexuality in World Cinema. Metuchen, NJ: The Scarecrow Press, 1983. 1535p. (2 vol.). $95.00. ISBN 8-8108-1609-1.
This two volume set alphabetically lists hundreds of films from the gamut of cinema genres and briefly describes the sexual nature of these movies. Standard as well as porno movies are included. The author's brief comments are informative, but fail to provide a rounded portrait of the movies discussed.

McCarthy, Todd, and Charles Flynn, ed. Kings of the Bs.
New York: E.B. Dutton, 1975. 561p. il. $6.95. ISBN
0-525-47378-5.
Lightly illustrated tome which covers various aspects
of low buget film making with essays by writers such as Manny
Farber, Andrew Sarris, Richard Thompson, Roger Ebert and the
editors. Films like *Thunder Road*, *Nightmare Alley*, and *The
Phoenix City Story* are dissected and several interviews are
included, among them with Samuel Z. Arkoff, Steve Broidy,
William Castle, Roger Corman, Joseph Kane, Arthur Lubin,
Edgar G. Ulmer, and Albert Zugsmith. Also included is a
useful filmography of 325 American directors.

McGee, Mark Thomas. Fast and Furious: The Story of
American International Pictures. Jefferson, NC: McFarland,
1984. 264p. $17.95. ISBN 0-89950-091-9.
The history of American International Pictures is told
in this readable text which includes the studios' beginnings,
its movies and such craftsmen as Alex Gordon, Edward L.
Cahn, Bert I. Gordon, Roger Corman, and Sidney Pink. The
studio's involvement in horror pictures is covered as its
working in other genres like sword and sandal, beach party,
and protest pictures. Biographies of studio personnel are
provided, as is a filmography. Updated by the same author
as *Faster and Furiouser: The Revised and Fattened Fable
of American International Pictures* (Jefferson, NC: McFarland,
1196. 360p. $40.00. ISBN 0-7864-0137-0).

McGee, Mark Thomas, and R.J. Robertson. The J.D.
Films: Juvenile Delinquency in the Movies. Jefferson, NC:
McFarland, 1982. 197p. il. $15.95 pap. ISBN 0089950-038-2.
Juvenile delinquency movies are given thorough coverage
in this book which has its main emphasis on the films of the
1950s, 1960s and early 1970s. Stars like Marlon Brando and
James Dean are examined as is film fare involving sex, drugs
and rock 'n' roll. Nicely illustrated, the volume also includes
a filmography.

Meyers, Richard. For One Week Only: The World of
Exploitation Films. Piscataway, NJ: New Century Publishers,
1983. 270p. il. $12.95 pap. ISBN 0-8329-0142-3.
Fun coverage of low budget exploitation from the 1960s
into the early 1980s. Individual films and genres are explored
under the umbrella chapters of sex, drugs and rock 'n' roll,
violence, and horror. The book is also filled with scores of
interesting photos and poster reproductions.

Miller, Don. B Movies. New York: Curtis Books, 1973.
350p. $1.50 pap.
This informal survey of the American low budget film from
the beginning of the sound era until the end of World War II is
one of the most readable and informative volumes written on
movies of that period. The author authoritatively looks at
hundreds of low budget movies, their makers and stars, and the
companies which produced them. Must reading for all fans of
B pictures.

Okuda, Ted, with Edward Watz. The Columbia Comedy
Shorts: Two-Reel Hollywood Film Comedies, 1933-1958.
Jefferson, NC: McFarland, 1986. 272p. $38.50. ISBN
0-89950-181-8.
One of the best books ever written about the field of
comedy short subjects, this volume covers the output of
Columbia Pictures. Highly informative, the book delves into
the history of its subjects, important directors and writers, and
the studio's various series. Among the latter, coverage is given
on such stars as The Three Stooges, Andy Clyde, Harry Langdon,
Charley Chase, Buster Keaton, Leon Errol, and Smith & Dale.
Filmographies are provided, as are selected personnel biographies.
Reissued in a softbound edition (Jefferson, NC: McFarland
Classics, 1998. 272p. $25.00 pap. ISBN 0-7864-0577-5).

Parish, James Robert. Ghosts and Angels in Hollywood
Films. Jefferson, NC: McFarland, 1994. 419p. il. $49.95.
ISBN 0-89950-676-3.
Casts and credits, a plot synopsis, and critical anaylsis
make up the ingredients for the discussion of 264 theatrical and
TV movies dealing with ghosts and angels. As the title implies,
only Hollywood-oriented productions are included, thus robbing
the book of some interesting titles, especially from Europe and
Asia. The films included, however, are discussed thoroughly, and
the book is well researched and enjoyable. It also contains 95
photographs and a film chronology of the included titles, all of
which were released between 1914 and 1991.

Parish, James Robert. Prostitution in Hollywood Films.
Jefferson, NC: McFarland, 1992. 593p. $49.95. ISBN
0-89950-677-1.
Plots, critiques, cast, and credits for some 389 films and
TV movies are included in this book, which ranges from silents
such as Theda Bara's *A Fool There Was* (1915) to 1991's *Whore*.
Hollywood's look at the world's oldest profession includes many

titles with the decades of the 1930s, 1960s, 1970s, and 1980s
being most prominent. Unlike other contemporary volumes, this
one also includes a number of titles from the silent era.

Ross, Jonathan. The Incredibly Strange Film Book. London:
Simon & Schuster, 1995. 324p. il. $24.95 pap. ISBN
0-671-71097-4.
Subtitled, "An Alternative History of the Cinema," this
oversized softbound volume discusses the world of the low
budget cinema worldwide. Divided into five parts, the author
first looks at cinema sex, including a history of porn movies,
Russ Meyer, and John Holmes. In the section on exploitation, he
looks at the movie *Maniac*, and the works of Edward D. Wood Jr.
Teenage and Drive-In Movies delves into these genres, along with
coverage of Mamie Van Doren's career. Rondo Hatton and
William Castle, and his film *The Tingler*, are discussed in
Gimmicks, and the volume closes with a look at horror movies
and violence. Well illustrated, the text is as fun as its subject.

Sennett, Ted. Warner Brothers Presents. New Rochelle,
NY: Arlington House, 1972. 428p. il. $11.95. ISBN
0-87000-136-1.
The history of the Warner Brothers studio, from the beginning
of the sound era with *Th Jazz Singer* in 1927 to 1949's *White
Heat*, is covered in this heavily illustrated volume. Since Warners
released many films in differing genres, the book provides chapters
on crime and social dramas, musicals, adventure films, comedies,
sob stories, melodramas and mysteries, war films, and biographies.
Brief biographies of studio stars and personnel are included, as is
a list of studio awards and a filmography.

Slide, Anthony. Aspects of American Film History Prior
to 1920. Metuchen, NJ: Scarecrow Press, 1978. 173p. $7.50.
ISBN 0-1808-1130-8.
This slim volume is packed with information on various aspects of
movie making in the first two decades of this century. The careers
of directors Colin Campbell, J. Searle Dawley, Victor Heerman, and
Edward Sloman are discussed, as are those of actress Ethel Grandin,
an early star for Universal, and Thomas H. Ince. Early film magazines
are discussed, in addition to the Thanhouser and Paralta companies.
Includes bibliographies for the Balboa, Biograph, Edison, Essanay,
Kalem, Lubin, Paralta, Selig, and Thanhouser companies.

Slide, Anthony, and Gevinson, Alan. The Big V: A History of
the Vitagraph Company. Metuchen, NJ: Scarecrow Press, 1987.
356p. $29.50. ISBN 0-81-8-2030-7.

This is a revised edition of a work first published by Scarecrow Press in 1976. The volume documents the history and the films of the Vitagraph Company, one of the most important of early production companies. Also included are player biographies and a filmography of all Vitagraph releases from 1898 through 1926. A very valuable reference tool.

Slide, Anthony. Early American Cinema. New York: A.S. Barnes, 1970. 192p. $2.95 pap. ISBN 0-498-07717-9.
Extreme ly entertaining and thoroughly researched volume on the history of the early days of the movies with chapters on such studios as Edison, Lubin, Vitagraph, Kalem, Essanay, Biograph, and Keystone. D.W. Griffith, Mack Sennett and the serial of Pearl White are also highlighted. A very important work on the cinema's infancy.

Slide, Anthony. The Kindergarten of the Movies: A History of the Fine Arts Company. Metuchen, NJ: Scarecrow Press, 1980. 246p. $13.50. ISBN 0-8108-1358-0.
D.W. Griffith headed the Fine Arts Company which was in operation from 1915 to 1917, not only making Griffith's films but also introducing Douglas Fairbanks and Erich von Stroheim. The volume discusses the company and its movies, and provides player biographies, a filmography, and commentary on the company's greatest accomplishment, *Intolerance*.

Taylor, Deems, Marcelene Peterson, and Bryant Hale. A Pictorial History of the Movies. New York: Simon and Schuster, 1949. 375p. il. $60.00.
First published in 1943, and later revised and enlarged, this is a landmark volume in the study of the cinema in a mass market format. Hundreds of photos, all informatively captioned, trace the history of the movies from its infancy through the 1940s.

Turner, George E., and Michael H. Price. Human Monsters: The Bizarre Psychology of Movie Villains. Northhampton, MA: Kitchen Sink Press, 1995. 208p. il. $16.95 pap. ISBN 0-87816-377-8.
A look at some of the most popular movie villains of the 1930s and 1940s is provided in this book which discusses a number of interesting features from various genres. Among them are *Svengali* (1931), *Mystery Ranch* (1932), *The Mystery of Edwin Drood* (1935), *Dark Eyes of London* (!939), *The Man Who Wouldn't Die* (1942), *The Seventh Victim* (1943), *So Dark The Night* (1946), and *Behind Locked Doors* (1948). Well written, very informative and nicely illustrated.

Tuska, Jon. The Vanishing Legion: A History of Mascot
Pictures, 1927-1935. Jefferson, NC: McFarland, 1982. 224p.
il. $17.95. ISBN 0-89550-030-7.
A thorough history of Nat Levine's Mascot Pictures with
a discussion of its serials and features along with stars like
Ken Maynard, Tom Mix, Bela Lugosi, and Gene Autry.
Nicely illustrated, the volume includes serial and feature
filmgraphies. The only drawback is the author's penchant
for the psychological in dealing with the studio's basically
tried-and-true plots.

Van Hise, James. Hot Blooded Dinosaur Movies. Las
Vegas, NV: Pioneer Books, 1993. 178p. il. $14.95 pap.
ISBN 1-55698-365-4.
Fairly interesting history of dinosaurs in movies from
Gertie the Dinosaur in the early silent days to *Jurassic Park*.
Along the way such films as *The Lost World* (1925), *King
Kong* (1933), *Godzilla* (1956), and *Journey to the Center of
The Earth* (1959) are highlighted as is the animation work
of such craftsmen as Willis O'Brien and Ray Harryhausen.
Okay volume for fans of dinosaur movies.

Walker, Mark. Ghostmasters. Boca Raton, FL: Cool
Hand Communications, 1994. 176p. il. $29.95. ISBN
1-56790-146-8.
While not dealing specifically with motion pictures, this
volume does thoroughly cover an offshoot of the industry: the
numerous midnight spook shows which were staged from the
1930s into the 1960s and were especially popular during the
1940s. Beautifully illustrated, the volume covers the various
ghost and horror shows and stars Sidney Boscart, Herman
Weber, Ray-Mond, George Marquis, Dr. Silkini, Bill Neff,
Donna Haynes, Bob Nelson, Philip Morris, Kara-Kum,
McCarl Roberts, and magicians such as Dantini. Even film
stars like Bela Lugosi and Glenn Strange are included since
they participated in theatrical spook shows. The book
provides very interesting coverage of a lost part of film
culture.

Whitcombe, Rick Trader. Savage Cinema. New York:
Bounty Books, 1975. 95p. il. $2.95 pap. ISBN
0-517-524236.
The cinema of violence is explored in this work which
includes a potpourri of themes and movie titles, ranging
from genres like the horror film and western to the works

of directors such as Alfred Hitchcock, Roman Polanski, and Stanley Kubrick. The book is also heavily illustrated with stills, most of which match its title.

Wilson, Arthur, ed. The Warner Bros. Golden Anniversary. New York: Dell Special, 1973. 192p. il. $2.95 pap.
Published as a part of Warner Bros.' 50th anniversary celebration, this oversized paperback provides cast and credits (although perfunctory for silents) for all of the company's releases from 1923-73. Sprinkled with pictures, the volume also includes Arthur Knight's essay on Warners' history.

Wortley, Richard. Erotic Movies. New York: Crescent Books, 1975. 140p. il. ISBN 0-517-16826X.
More than 200 stills, many of them containing nudity, illustrate this work on the history of sex in the cinema. Going back to the cinema's earliest days, the author traces eroticism in the movies up to the mid-1970s. The author emphasizes that the work is a hopefully amusing and lightweight account of its subject.

--British Films

Barr, Charles. All Our Yesterdays: 90 Years of British Cinema. London: British Film Institute, 1986. 446p. $7.95 pap. ISBN 0-815170-179-5.
The history of the British cinema is presented in a series of essays which range from a look at the beginnings of the movies in the British Isles, the industry's troubled relations with the government, the relationship between cinema and literature, stage, music halls, radio and television, the major film companies and independents, and various film genres like the documentary film, drama, comedy and animation. Stars Diana Dors, Paul Robeson, and Dirk Bogarde are profiled. The book contains a useful filmography of movies discussed in the text. A recommended look at the history of English cinema.

Gifford, Denis. British Cinema: An Illustrated Guide. New York: A.S. Barnes, 1968. 176p. il. $1.95 pap.
Illustrated filmographies of nearly 550 British movie personnel with brief biographie s and a listing of their fims with release years. The index lists all the films mentioned in the text cross referenced by entry number. A very useful guide for researchers.

Maxford, Howard. Hammer, House of Horror: Behind
the Screams. Woodstock, NY: Overlook Press, 1996. 192p.
il. ISBN 0-87951-652-6.
An accounting of the movies of the British film studio
which produced a series of glossy horror movies from the
mid-1950s into the 1970s, the volume is well researched and
covers its subject in thorough fashion. Studies Hammer
from its beginnings with the release *of The Mystery of the
Marie Celeste* (1935), starring Bela Lugosi, to its heyday
in the 1950s and 1960s with stylish horror vehicles featuring
Peter Cushing and Christopher Lee. While the layout is not
reader friendly, the book includes quality illustrations (some
in color), a who's who of key personnel, and a filmography.

Quinlan, David. British Sound Films: The Studio Years.
Totowa, N.J.: Barnes & Noble, 1984. 407p. il. $30.00. ISBN
0-389-20539-7.
Author David Quinlan has succinctly covered the hundreds
of British feature films released from the beginning of the
sound era through 1959. There is a thumbnail description of
each title, including cast and credits, plot and critial comment.
The author certainly knows his subject and it shows in this
exceedingly valuable research tool, which is also fun reading.
At the end of each decade covered is a list of short subjects
issued during that time period. The author also provides
coverage of the main star and film for each decade.

--Italian Films

Lephrohon, Pierre. The Italian Cinema. New York:
Praeger, 1972. 256p. il. 4.95 pap.
First published in Italy in 1966 as *Le Cinema Italien*,
this informative volume covers the history of Italian movies
from 1895 through the 1960s. After a brief look at the
formative years of Italian cinema, the author discusses the
golden era of silent films, the decline of the 1920s, movies
under fascism, the rise of neo-realism, and the 1960s output.
Also includes a chapter on important directors and a
biographical dictionary.

Staig, Laurence, and Williams, Tony. Italian Western:
The Opera of Violence. London: Odeon, 1975. 191p. il.
$5.95 pap. ISBN 0-85647-059-7.
One of the first, and best, studies of the European Western,
this volume covers numerous films, stars, and directors

as it discusses the popularity of the genre and its many renderings. Covered in detail are the works of director Sergio Leone and composer Ennio Morricone. Heavily illustrated, the book also includes biographies of several composers and a filmography.

HANDBOOKS--TELEVISION

General

Burke, David. Street Talk -2-: Slang Used by Teens, Rappers, Surfers, and Popular American Television Shows. Illustrated by Jim Graul. Optime Books, 1992. 286p. $16.95 pap. ISBN 1879440067.
While television does not constitute the central focus of this source, the medium's contribution to the vernacular of the youth subculture is clearly documented. The text is arranged alphabetically by term.

Carter, T. Batn, Marc A. Franklin, and Jay B. Wright. The First Amendment and the Fifth Estate: Regulation of Electronic Mass Media. 3rd ed. Minola, NY: Foundation Press, 1988. 635p.
Analyzes the laws and regulations governing the electronic mass media as well as the policies underlying these legal precedents. Chapters include The Spectrum and Its Utilization, Justifications for Government Regulation, Broadcast Licensing, Media Concentration, Legal Control of Broadcast Programming (Political Speech, Nonpolitical Speech), Noncommercial Broadcasting, Cable Television, New Communications Technologies, Copyright and Trademark, Defamation, Privacy, and Special Problems of Electronic Media Journalists.

Dyja, Eddie. BFI Film and Television Handbook 1997. British Film Institute, 1998. $35.00 pap. ISBN 0851706371.

The Editors of TV Guide. The TV Guide Book of Lists. New York: Harper Collins, 1998. 224p. $5.99 pap. ISBN 006101091X.
An assemblage of lists relating to television programming and personalities since the late 1940s. The lists emphasize provocative issues over the straightforward presentation of facts; e.g., the greatest cliff- hanger, the worst talk show host, stars who have doubled as singers.

Frank, Sam. Buyer's Guide to 50 Years of TV on Video. Prometheus Books, 1998. 1498p. $22.95 pap. ISBN 1573922269.
The work lists all television programs from 1949 to 1998 available on prerecorded video formats. The scope encompasses more than 50,00 shows, including a wide range of sitcoms; dramatic series and anthologies; science fiction, westerns, variety shows, game shows, children's programming, specials, and documentaries. The inclusion of much factual material in addition to the basics of locating a purchase source may prove

confusing to some users; e.g., failure to highlight the coding of video vendors necessitates considerable searching to locate the necessary code for conversion into a telephone or mail order firm.

Gelfand, Steve. Television Theme Recordings: An Illustrated Discography, 1951-1994. Ann Arbor, MI: Popular Culture, Ink, 1994. 332p. il. composer, popular recording artist, and song title indexes. ISBN 1-56075-021-9.
The author succeeds in his effort to compile the most informative reference source ever regarding TV theme music. Arranged alphabetically by program title, each entry includes series title, theme number (i.e., when different themes were used for a series) and dates, theme title, composers, supernumeraries, recording artist, recording format, record title, record label and number, re- issue status, use of previously released recording, relationship to themes from other media,, public domain and classical compositions, release date of record, different versions by same artist, and instrumental/vocal designations. These data fields--as well as other forms of notations (e.g., abbreviations) are discussed in an exhaustive introduction. The text is complemented by the following appendixes: I. Top Ten Most Recorded TV Themes; II. Composers of the Most Number of Different Recorded TV Themes; III. Charted TV Themes; IV. Not TV Themes; V. Themes Recorded by a Cast Member of a Series; VI. Recorded Themes Used for Sequels, Revivals, Spin-offs, etc.; VII. A Basic LP Collection; VIII. Grammy Award Winners; and IX. Historical Reprints: "Music for Young Killers" and "Name That TV Tune." Also includes a Selective Foreign Discography.

Gelman, Morrie, and Gene Accas. The Best in Television: 50 Years of Emmys. Genl Publishing Group, 1998. 288p. index. $35.00. ISBN 1575440423.
Lists all Emmy winners by category for each year since the inception of the award. Includes a historical overview of the Emmys which notes its influence on the development of the television medium.

Jarvis, Everett Grant, and Lois Johe. Final Curtain: Deaths of Noted Movie and Television Personalities. 9th ed. Carol Publishing Group, 1998. 448p. il. $24.95 pap. ISBN 0806520582.
An inventory of more than 8,800 film and television celebrities arranged by year of death with further subdivisions both chronologically and alphabetically by last name. Entries usually provide the cause of death, the actor's birthname, Oscar nominations/ awards, and names of spouses. Includes a directory of burial places, organized by state and city, and a statistical breakdown of deaths, ages, and frequency of causes.

Jarvis, Robert M., and Paul R. Joseph, editors. Prime Time Law: Fictional Television as Legal Narrative. Carolina Academic Press, 1998. 336p. $32.50. ISBN 0890898057. Also available in paperback edition.
Featuring contributions from academicians in communications and technology, English, history, law, political science, and other germane fields, the book focuses on the depiction of legal issues and the legal profession in fictional televis ion. More than 350 programs have been cited in the text.

Javna, John. The TV Theme Song Sing-along Songbook. Designed by Roland Addad. New York: St. Martin's, 1984. 128p. $7.95 pap. ISBN 0312782152.
Unabashed in its commitment to reviving old memories, the book reproduces the music and lyrics to many of the most popular television theme songs of television first four decades.

Kraeuter, David W. Radio and Television Pioneers: A Patent Bibliography. Metuchen, NJ: Scarecrow, 1992. 319p. index. $35.00. ISBN 0-8108-2556-2.
The work includes, under inventor name, a chronologically arranged listing of awarded patents. Each entry is appended by a citation (noting name of device, patent number, date, volume, and page) which facilitates location in the *Official Gazette of the Patent Office*. The patents can generally be found through utilization of the patent number in patent depository libraries. The scope is limited to U.S. patents.

Lance, Steven. Written Out of Television: A TV Lover's Guide to Cast Changes 1945-1994. Lanham, MD: Madison Books/University Press of America; distr., National Book Network, 1996. 507p. il. index. $24.95 pap. ISBN 1-56833-071-5.
The source has mixed success in achieving its stated goal of providing "the most accurate and detailed information ever available...about the programs where actors have been written out." Similarly, the entries range widely with respect to quality; some feature insightful discussions of the factors behind cast changes whereas others are marred by poorly plot summaries and omissions of key cast developments; e.g., while a comprehensive list of crew members of the Starship *Enterprise* has been provided for *Star Trek* enthusiasts, no mention is made of Edith Bunker's death on *All in the Family*.

Lentz, Harris M., III, comp. Western and Frontier Film and Television Credits 1903-1995. 2 volumes. Jefferson, NC: McFarland, 1996. Film and television indexes. $175.00/set. ISBN 0-7864-0158-3.
Lentz already possesses firm credentials within this field, having earned considerable Praise for his 1983 publication, *Science Fiction, Horror & Fantasy Film and Television Credits*, and its 1989 and 1994 supplements. Volume 1 covers the actors/actresses, directors, producers, and writers contributing to motion picture and TV series. The entries--arranged alphabetically by last name--include birth and death dates as well as a chronological listing of film credits (which cite title, date, and for actors, character names). Volume 2 consists of both film and television indexes; the latter lists all Western series broadcast up through June 1995, incorporating notation of regular cast and an episode index that refers to the individual show's title, original air date, cast, and character names.

Letterman, David, and Steve O'Donnell. The Last Night with David Letterman Book of Top Ten Lists. New York: Pocket Books, 1990. 160p. il. $12.00 pap. ISBN 0671726714.
David Letterman late, late night program, in the time slot immediately following Johnny Carson's *Late Night* on NBC, was a cult favorite during the 1980s. This source

has compiled 175 of the more outrageous of Letterman's Top Ten Lists, a popular staple of the show.

Northam, Mark, and Lisa Anne Miller. Film and Television Composer's Resource Guide. Hal Leonard Publishing, 1998. 198p. $34.95 spiral binding. ISBN 0793595614. Provides information germane both to composing per se and the process of finding work within the film and television industries.

Orion BlueBook: Video & Television 1999. Annual. Orion Research, 1998. $144.00. ISBN 0932089968.

Parish, James Robert, and Vincent Terrace. The Complete Actors' Television Credits, 1948-1988. 2 volumes. 2nd ed. Metuchen, NJ: Scarecrow, 1989-1990. il. ISBN 0-8108-2204-0 (v. 1); 0-8108-2258-X (v. 2).
Arranged by actor (volume 1) and actress (volume 2), the work's entries incorporate all entertainment programs broadcast on network and cable television in addition to those produced for syndication.

Rettenmund, Matthew. Totally Awesome 80s: A Lexicon of the Music, Videos, Movies, TV Show Stars, and Trends of That Decadent Decade. New York: St. Martin's Press, 1997. 224p. il. $15.95 pap. ISBN 0312144369.
Television programs and stars share the spotlight with popular music, video clips, celebrities, fads (e.g., skinny ties, Valspeak), fashions, entertainment films, toys, and other cultural artifacts in defining the "Greed Decade." The breezy text is augmented by splashy layouts and some 300 photos.

Warren, Albert, ed. Television and Cable Factbook 1999. 3 Volumes. Warren Publishing, 1999. $525.00 pap. ISBN 157696020X.

Historical and Sociological Surveys

Abt, Vicki, and Leonard Mustazza. Coming After Oprah: Cultural Fallout in the Age of the TV Talk Show. Bowling Green, OH: Bowling Green State University, 1997. $48.95. ISBN 0879727519. Also available in paperback edition.
Refuting arguments that the TV talk shows are little more than harmless entertainment, the authors examine the historical development and cultural significance of the genre. The first half of the work explores the mechanics of the talk-show universe, while the latter portion looks at the behind-the-scenes economic maneuvering and their implications. The corporate and political interests involved are also noted. Abt and Mustazza, both professors at Pennsylvania State University's Abington College, conclude the study with recommendations as to how society can protect itself from the genre's inherent deceptions and misinformation.

Baker, William F., George Dessart, and Bill Moyers. Down the Tube: An Inside Account of the Failure of American Television. Basic Books, 1999. 352p. $14.00 pap. ISBN 0465007236.

The book argues that television, which originally promised to enrich citizens by offering easy access to quality entertainment and the latest news and information, has developed into an assembly line--fueled by a communications industry that equates viewers with demographic statistics--producing drivel pandering to base interests. Without providing substantive solutions to this dilemma, the authors relate the decline in quality of TV programming to the cycles of government regulation and deregulation that ensue from the ever changing U.S. political environment. Baker has been a high- level executive in both public and commercial television, Dessart--now an academic--was a former vice president at CBS, and Moyers has been active within the medium as a writer, producer, and on-screen journalist.

Boddy, William. Fifties Television: The Industry and Its Critics. Reprint ed. Champagne, IL: University of Illinois Press, 1992. (Illinois Studies in Communication) $16.95 pap. ISBN 025206299X.
The title is somewhat misleading in that the work focuses on the early developmental stages of the TV industry, encompassing the technological innovations prior to post-World War II era, the regulatory conflicts of the 1940s, and the economic expansion and programming upheavals of the 1950s.

Brinkley, Joel. Defining Vision: The Battle for the Future of Television. New York: Harcourt Brace, 1997. 352p. $27.00. ISBN 0151000875. Also available in paperback edition.
Chronicles the embryonic stages of high-definition, all-digital TV in the U.S. According to General Computing, the work effectively relates "how this multibillion dollar business was conceived; why cynical broadcasters jumped on the bandwagon; how a competing Japanese standard sent Congress into a panic; how U.S. companies researched, jockeyed, lobbied, spied, and bribed to set the HDTV standard; and how the government's tax greed almost unraveled the whole mess after a decade of expensive development."

Chiu, Tony. CBS: The First 50 Years. General Publishing Group, 1998. 304p. $35.00. ISBN 1575440830. Also available in paperback edition.
This work focuses on the network's television division with little more than passing mention of its accomplishments in radio, the record industry, or related entertainment endeavors. Chiu has produced an appealing popular history rather than an insider's accounts of events at the Big Rock.

D'Acci, Julie. Defining Women: Television and the Case of Cagney & Lacey. Chapel Hill, NC: University of North Carolina Press, 1994. $49.95. ISBN 0807821322. Also available in paperback edition.
D'Acci examines the extent to which this popular 1980s program reflected the changing roles of women in American society.

Fourie, Pieter J., ed. Critical Television Analyses; An Introduction. Juta and Co., 1994. $29.00. ISBN 0702124877.

Frantzich, Stephen, and John Sullivan. The C-Span Revolution. Norman, OK: University of Oklahoma Press, 1999. 448p. $14.95 pap. ISBN 0806131306; hardcover edition, 1996. $24.95. ISBN 0806128704.
A thoroughly researched history of the Cable-Satellite Public Affairs Network which focuses on the relationship between the political arena and the media's role in disseminating information about this process. Covers the origins of the network, its corporate culture, its influence on society, and its probable role in the future "Age of Cyberdemocracy."

Greenfield, Jeff. Television: The First Fifty Years. New York: Crescent, 1981. 248p. index, bibl. il. ISBN 0-517-328186.
Greenfield not only documents the evolution of the medium, he analyzes the causes and effects of television's vast power and influence, the factors which render advertising so effective, the reasons certain programs thrive--and others fall by the wayside, and the particular impact TV has had upon youth who have grown up viewing it. The narrative is divided into the following sections: Television Comes to America, Prime Time, Advertising, Daytime, News and Sports, and The Next Generation. The 473 photographs--48 in full color--greatly enhance the work's appeal.

Hendershot, Heather. Saturday Morning Censors: Television Regulation Before the V-Chip (Console-Ing Passions). Durham, NC: Duke University Press, 1999. 296p. $17.95 pap. ISBN 0822322404. Also available in hardcover edition.

Henry, Judith, and Edith M. Pavese. TV Mania: A Timeline of Television. New York: Henry N. Abram, 1998. 144p. il. $12.95. ISBN 0810938928.
Provides an encapsulated his tory chronologically beginning with the pioneering era of broadcasting. The concise factual entries are augmented by 185 illustrations, 60 of which are in color.

Hinds, Lynn Boyd. Broadcasting the Local News: The Early Years of Pittsburgh's KDTV-TV. Pennsylvania State University Press, 1995. 173p. 18.95 pap. ISBN 0271014393.
In addition to documenting the history of the city's first television station, the work provides a close-up picture of how television journalism operated during these developmental years. These insights should prove particularly useful to aspiring television journalists/producers/engineers.

Marc, David, and David Bianculi. Comic Visions: Television Comedy and American Culture. 2nd ed. Blackwell Publishing, 1997. 256p. $23.95 pap. ISBN 1577180038.

Marc, David, and Horace Newcomb. Demographic Vistas: Television in American Culture. Rev. ed. Philadelphia: University of Pennsylvania Press, 1996. 240p. $17.95 pap. ISBN 0812215605.

Marling, Karal Ann. As Seen on TV: The Visual Culture of Everyday Life in the 1950s. Cambridge, MA: Harvard University Press, 1994. 328p. il. $24.95. ISBN 0674048822.
Marling, a professor of Art History and American Studies at the University of Minnesota, combines insightful social commentary with a breezy writing style geared to the lay reader. She focuses on the rise of television and its impact on American life. Themes analyzed include the national obsession with Mamie Eisenhower's hair and clothing, the marketing of Disneyland, the psychosexual lure of chrome- laden cars, and the increasing hegemony of design over function in the development of American products.

MacGregor, Brent. Live, Direct and Biased?: Making Television News in the Satellite Age. Edward Arnold, 1997. $60.00. ISBN 0340662247. Also available in paperback edition.
Surveys the evolution of TV news, including an accelerated cycle, a greater reliance on technology, and an increasing preoccupation with the bottom line. MacGregor argues that the decisions made by the news media on a daily basis frequently undercut its information dissemination function.

MacNeil, Robert. The People Machine. New York: Harper & Row, 1968.
MacNeil, a longtime television journalist, provides an insightful look at the medium's effect on politics and public attitudes.

Minow, Newton N., with Craig Lamay. Abandoned in the Wasteland: Children, Television, and the First Amendment. Hill & Wang, 1996. $11.00 pap. ISBN 0809015897.
Argues that the First Amendment can be a tool to ensue that television is a positive, rather than a negative, force in childhood development. Lamay and Minow, FCC chairman in the early 1960s famed for his "television is a cultural wasteland" speech, survey the eolution of the medium and offer recommendations for a policy to limit the commercial interests that presently control programming.

Monaco, Paul. Understanding Society, Culture, and Television. Westport, CT: Praeger, 1998. 152p. index, bibl. $55.00. ISBN 0-275-9-657-9.
Monaco, a professor at Montana State University, attempts to ascertain the impact of television on contemporary society and culture. He argues that the medium can be understood only be viewing it as an art form, and measuring its role in concert with the "first principles of human reason and liberty."

Mullan, Bob. Consuming Television: Television and Its Audience. Blackwell, 1997. 256p. $25.95 pap. ISBN 063120234X. Also available in a hardcover edition.
Mullan utilizes a strong sociological slant in examining the interrelationship between the TV industry and its viewing public.

Newman, Jay. Religion vs. Television. New York: Praeger, 1996. 155p. $55.00. ISBN 0275956407.

Examines the competitive relationship between religion and television as well as positive and negative impacts of this situation on cultural affairs. Recommended as a core readin source for students and academics within the fields of religion, cultural studies, communications technology, and philosophy.

Pavese, Edith M., and Judith Henry. TV Mania: A Timeline of Television. New York: Harry N. Abrams, 1998. 144p. il. $12.95. ISBN 0810938928.
Outlines TV history from the pioneer era to the present day. The concise factual mode of presentation is complemented by 185 illustrations, 60 of which are in color.

Roman, James. Love, Light, and a Dream: Television's Past, Present, and Future. Westport, CT: Praeger, 1998. 320p. index, bibl. $24.95 pap. ISBN 0-275-96437-X. Roman, associate professor of Media Studies at Hunter College, examines the forces which have lead to present day stature of television as a social and cultural vehicle. Covers the Federal Communications Commission's role as a regulatory body, the relationship between cable services and telephone systems as information providers, television advertising campaigns and the structure of the agency business, the challenges faced by public broadcasting, and the dynamics of TV news and the creation of a journalistic mythology.

Shulman, Arthur, and Roger Youman. How Sweet It Was. New York: Shorecrest, 1966. il.
This source remains unparalleled in its coverage of the first twenty years of commercial broadcasting. The engaging text is complemented by a fascinating array of 1,500-odd photographs.

Skutch, Ira, ed. The Days of Live: Television's Golden Age As Seen by 21 Directors Guild of America Members. Lanham, MD: Scarecrow Press, 1998. (Directors Guild of America Oral History Series, No. 16) $26.00 pap. ISBN 0810834928.

Walker, James R., and Douglas A. Ferguson. The Broadcast Television Industry. Allyn & Bacon, 1998. 200p. $30.75 pap. ISBN 0205189504.
Surveys the history and current practices of commercial and public television, including coverage of regulatory issues, the operation of local stations and national networks, audience research, the cultural and economic impact of the medium, and the future of broadcasting as a force for TV dissemination in the face of new competing forces.

Watson, Mary Ann. The Expanding Vista: American Television in the Kennedy Years. Reprint ed. Durham, NC: Duke University Press, 1994. 273p. $17.95 pap. ISBN 0822314436. Originally published in 1990 by the Oxford University Press. Examines the promise of the medium as a leader in disseminating information and culture during its second decade as a large-scale commercial entity.

Watson, Mary Ann, Gerald D. Nash, and Richard W. Etulain. Defining Visions: Television and the American Experience Since 1945. New York: HBJ College and School Division, 1997. 288p. $25.00 pap. ISBN 0155032011.

Zook, Kristal Brent. Color by Fox: The Fox Network and the Revolution in Black Television. Oxford, UK: Oxford University Press, 1999. 160p. $14.95 pap. ISBN 0195106121.
The work argues that ethnicity, gender, and race represent marketable commodities in the eyes of TV executives. Zook, a media columnist with the hip-hop periodical, *The Source*, illustrates how Fox established a foothold in the marketplace by flooding the airwaves with programming geared largely to black viewers such as *Living Single*, *Martin*, and *Roc*. She notes that these and other "issue-oriented" programs were dropped once mainstream success appeared imminent for the network. This formula went on to become the model for other fledgling networks, most notably Warner Bros. and United Paramount.

Programming

Baxter, Joan. Television Musicals: Plots, Critiques, Casts and Credits for 222 Shows Written for and Presented on Television, 1944-1996. Jefferson, NC: McFarland, 1997. 216p. $45.00 (library binding). ISBN 0786402865.
The works covered include musical episodes from nonmusical shows, animated specials, and operas and related works commissioned for the small screen. Each entry provides air date, network, running time, cast and credits, a song listing, plot synopsis (the show itself and, where applicable, the story from which it was adapted), award nominations (and awards won), recordings, videos, published music, and contemporary reviews of the show.

Brooks, Tim, and Earle Marsh. The Complete Directory to Prime Time Network TV Shows, 1946-Present. 5th ed., completely rev. and updated. New York: Ballantine, c1992. 1207p. il., name index.
Includes programs airing during prime time ("roughly 7:30-11:00 p.m., E.S.T."), late night network shows, and top syndicated fare broadcast primarily in the evening. Entries, arranged by title of series, provide inclusive dates of telecasting, program history, cast members (both regulars and high profile guests), plot commentary, and noteworthy episodes. The text is complemented by many useful appendixes; e.g., prime time schedules, 1946-1991, Emmy Award winners, top-rated programs by season, spin-offs, series hit theme recordings.

Brooks, Tim, and Earle Marsh. The Complete Directory to Prime Time Network and Cable TV Shows 1946-Present. 6th ed., revised. New York: Ballantine, 1995. il., name index.
Publicity notes that the work has received its most sweeping revision in more than decade. Upgrades include extensive cable coverage (over 150 entries), 300 new network and syndicated listings, 300-odd updated listings of continuing shows, an all-time Top 100 programs list, an expanded index of more than 15,000 personalities, and logs for the

new Paramount and Warner Brothers networks. Among the special features are annual breakdowns for program schedules spanning forty- nine years, top-rated shows per season, Emmy Award winners, longest running series, spinoff series, theme songs, and a history of the "Seven Era" of TV programmimg.

Castleman, Harry, and Walter J. Podrazik. Harry and Wally's Favorite TV Shows. New York: Prentice-Hall, 1989. 628p. performer index. ISBN 0-13-933250-2. The book includes over 2,100 programs arranged alphabetically by title. The shows are rated on a zero-to- four scale; additional data includes original air date, number of episodes, producer, and stars. Applicable entries refe r the user to a home video section. Both "contemporary" material and reruns are covered; prime-time comedy and drama series receive greater attention than variety, game, and talk shows. Soap operas and children's programs are omitted altogether.

Davis, Mitchell P, ed. Talk Show Selects 1998: A Guide to the Nation's Most Influential Television and Radio Talk Shows. Broadcast Interview Source, 1998. $185.00 (ringbound edition). ISBN 0934333319.

Einstein, Daniel. Special Edition: A Guide to Network Television Documentary Series and Special News Reports, 1955-1979. Metuchen, NJ: Scarecrow, 1987. 1051p. personality and production and technical personnel indexes. ISBN 0-8108-1898-1. Includes three major sections: commercial television documentary series, arranged by series title and date; a chronologically arranged listing of documentaries produced by David L. Wolper; and network news specials and special reports, by program date. The entries (covering 7,000 individual programs and over 120 series) include program title, a brief annotation, date, and subjects covered. The personality index incorporates interviewees and those profiled, while production and technical personnel index covers producers, journalists, and narrators.

Erickson, Hal. Syndicated Television: the First Forty Years, 1947-1987. Jefferson, NC: McFarland, 1989. 418p. index. individual and program name index. ISBN 0-89950-410-8.
According to the author's *Introduction*, the book delineates "programs either made exclusively for non-network play, or...programs perhaps intended for network telecasts but ultimately making their debuts in syndication." The entries are organized first by decade, then program type (e.g., adventure/mystery, game/quiz, religious, sports, talk/interview). Appended by an annotated bibliography.

Fantle, David. Classic TV: 50 Great Shows, 50 Theme Songs. Hal Leonard Publishing Company, 1996. $16.95 pap. ISBN 0793547628.

Gianakos, Larry James. Television Drama Series Programming: a Comprehensive Chronicle, 1947-1959. Metuchen, NJ: Scarecrow, 1980. 565p. index of series titles. The work, arranged by season, surveys drama series introduced during the season in question and lists episodes for that years (and subsequent seasons for continuing series). Episode data includes title, broadcast date, principal cast, and source (for adaptations).

The lead-in volume, chronologically speaking, of a series which includes the following titles:

_____, 1959-1975. 1978. 794p.
_____, 1975-1980. 1981. 457p.
_____, 1980-1982. 1983. 678p.
_____, 1982-1984. 1987. 830p.
_____, 1984-1986. 1992. 705p.

While the basic format has been retained, some notable changes have occurred in the midst of the series. Newer volumes list programs from earlier seasons that had been omitted and provide corrections and expansion of material in earlier volumes. Recent volumes have added credits for writers and directors and contain useful appendixes (e.g., teleplays adapted from Pulitzer Prize-winning works, Greek drama, Shakespeare, etc.).

Lentz, III, Harris M. Television Westerns Episode Guide: All United States Series, 1949-1996. Jefferson, NC: McFarland, 1997. 675p. index. $95.00 (library binding). ISBN 0786403772.
Includes 180 series going back to 1949, when *Hopalong Cassidy* and *The Lone Ranger* were first aired. The entries--arranged alphabetically by title--cite the broadcast history of the program, network affiliation, day and time slot, a list of regular cast members, a brief premise of the series, and an episode breakdown, which notes title, original air ate, leading guest stars, and a brief synopsis.

Lewis, Jon E., and Penny Stempel. Cult TV: The Comedies. Bay Books, 1998. 256p. il. $19.95 pap. ISBN 0912333650.
The work--arranged alphabetically by title--covers more than 300 comedies spanning television's first fifty years. Each entry includes features on cast members, production data, and behind-the-scenes information and anecdotes. The text is complemented by close to 100 black-and-white stills.

Marill, Alvin H. Movies Made for Television: the Telefeature and the Mini-Series, 1964-1986. New York: Zoetrope, c1987. 576p. il., producer, director, writer, and performer indexes.
Focuses on "nearly 2,100 films and mini-series made expressly for television"; continuing series lie outside the purview of this work. Arranged alphabetically by program title, the entries provide network affiliation, date(s) broadcast, production company, length, characters and cast, plot summary (with comment), and director, producer, teleplay author, photographer, etc., credits.

McNeil, Alex. Total Television: a Comprehensive Guide to Programming from 1948 to the Present. 3rd ed. New York: Penguin, 1991. 1142p. name index.
This source provides considerably less detail than *The Complete Directory to Prime Time Network TV Shows, 1946-Present* (c1992), by Tim Brooks and Earle Marsh for the majority of programs; however, it is preferable for the inclusion of daytime and public television series and its broader coverage of syndicated programs.

McNeil, Alex. Total Television: a Comprehensive Guide to Programming from 1948 to the Present. 4th ed. New York: Penguin, 1997. 1264p. name index. ISBN 01402667379 pap. Also available in CD-R format.
Information on 5,400 series--an their key participants--is presented in alphabetically arranged entries ranged from one to four pages in length. An appendix lists special broadcasts in chronological order. Reviews in the *Lost Angeles Times* and *Washington Post* refer to it as the "best written" and "more thorough directory" of its kind.

Rose, Brian G., ed. Robert S. Alley, advisory ed. TV Genres: A Handbook and Reference Guide. Westport, CT: Greenwood, 1985. ix, 453p. index. bibl., videography. ISBN 0-313-23724-7.
Specialists have explored the essential features of nineteen formats or styles of television programming (e.g., game shows, sitcoms, westerns). Each chapter includes a historical survey, an analysis of themes and issues, a bibliographc essay, and a videography.

Shapiro, Mitchell E. Television Network Daytime and Late-Night Programming, 1959-1989. Jefferson, NC: McFarland, 1990. 264p. il.
A companion edition to the author's *Television Network Prime-Time Programming, 1948-1988* (McFarland, 1989).

Shapiro, Mitchell E. Television Network Prime -Time Programming, 1948-1988. Jefferson, NC: McFarland, 1989. 743p. il. show title index. ISBN 0-89950-412-4.
Arranged chronologically, the source includes prime-time schedules (the 7-11 p.m. Eastern Standard Time period) on a month-by- month basis for all major networks: ABC, CBS, DuMont, Fox, and NBC. Also provides an in-depth compilation of Network programming moves such as series premieres, cancellations, and shifts in time slots in addition to an annual recap of key programming moves.

Shapiro, Mitchell E. Television Network Weekend Programming, 1959-1990. Jefferson, NC: McFarland, 1992. 464p. il.
The tool follows the same format as the author's *Television Network Prime-Time Programming, 1948-1988* (McFarland, 1990).

Story, David. America on the Rerun: V Shows That Never Die. Citadel Press, 1993. 239p. il. $16.95 pap. ISBN 0806514108.
Spotlights series that have enjoyed continued popularity in syndication; e.g., *The Brady Bunch, Get Smart, Gilligan's Island, Mr. Ed*. The separate section--each devoted to a different series--consist of plot synopses, anecdotes, interviews with cast members, and an abundance of program stills.

Terrace, Vincent. Fifty Years of Television: a Guide to Series and Pilots, 1937-1988. New York: Cornwall Books, 1991. 864p.
Comparable to *The Complete Directory to Prime Time Network TV Shows, 1946-Present* (c1992), by Tim Brooks and Earle Marsh--the reference standard in this field--with regard to overall coverage. Terrace's work lacks many of the appendixes contained

within Brooks and Marsh volume. However, Terrace is the preferred source for data on early programs and series pilots.

Waldron, Vince. Classic Sitcoms: A Celebration of the Best in Prime -Time Comedy. 2nd ed., revised and expanded. Silman-James Press, 1998. 560p. il. $18.95 pap. ISBN 1879505258.
Rather than attempting to compete with the all-inclusive programming guidebooks presently available, Waldron focuses on the most popular prime-time sitcoms of television's first fifty years as a viable commercial entity. He eschews the concise entries employed by Terrace, Brooks and Marsh, and others in favor of more thorough discussions of shows such as *The Honeymooners*, *Graucho*, *I Love Lucy*, *Happy Days*, *Laverne and Shirley*, and *Cheers*.

West, Richard. Television Westerns: Major and Minor Series, 1946-1978. Jefferson, NC: McFarland, 1987. 155p. il. index. ISBN 0-89950-252-0.
The book covers over 130 televsion series that premiered between 1946 and 1978. The chronologically arranged entries range in length from two paragraphs to several pages for the most popular series (e.g., *Bonanza*, *Gunsmoke*, *Rawhide*). They offer a menu of miscellaneous facts (dates and networks of original airing, performers, theme music, etc.), gossip, and subjective commentary. A valuable part of the work, the appendices list actors and names of characters they played; Emmy Award winners; ratings winners; titles under which shows played when rerun in syndication; and original network air times.

Woolery, George W. Animated TV Specials: the Complete Directory to the First Twenty-Five Years, 1962-1987. Metuchen, NJ: Scarecrow, 1989. 542p. il. distributor, studio/production company, producer, director, filmmaker, writer, musician and lyricist indexes. ISBN 0-8108-2198-2.
The work is devoted to "all special animated television presentations aired on the various networks or syndicated exclusively in the United States." The entries, arranged by program title, provides broadcast history, production credits, principal characters and voices, and plot summary. The appendices include listings of holiday and topical specials.

Woolery, George W. Children's Television: The First Thirty-Five Years, 1946-1981. 2 volumes. Metuchen, NJ: Scarecrow, 1983-1985. 788p. il. indexes. ISBN 0-8108-1651-2.
Covers animated cartoon, live, film, and tape series produced for children. The programs, organized alphabetically by title, provide run dates, production credits, cast members and voices, and notable episode data.

Woolery, Lynn, Robert W. Malsbary, and Robert G. Strange. Warner Bros. Television: Every Show of the Fifties and Sixties Episode -by-Episode. Jefferson, NC: McFarland, 1985. 296p. il. name index. ISBN 0-89950-144-3.
The book lists all Warner Brothers series alphabetically by title, followed by a chronological listing of aired episodes (each of which is annotated). Biographical

sketches of performers are also included. Although rather superficial in approach, first rate entertainment value can be found here.

--Great Britain

Baskin, Ellen. Serials on British Television 1950-1994. Brookfield, VT: Scholar Press/Ashgate Publishing, 1996. 332p. title, type, producer, director, cast member, location and era indexes. $69.95. ISBN 1-85928-015-3.
The work covers over 900 serials (defined by Baskin as "drama broadcast in a number of episodes telling one connected story" or a multipart, self-contained drama) up through early 1995. The entries--arranged by decade, with each serial in chronological order by first episode broadcast date--cite title, date and timing, television production company, availability on video, number of episodes, genre, location and timeframe of plot, producer, director, writer, book title and author on which book was based (where applicable), cast members, plot synopsis, and other notable data.

Vahimagi, Tise, comp. British Television: An Illustrated Guide. 2nd ed. London: Oxford University Press, 1996. 400p. $29.95. ISBN 0198159269.
Attempts to provide as complete a list as is possible of the more than 1,100 programs aired in Great Britain from 1936 to the mid-1990s. The chronologically arranged program entries--which include data comparable to the leading tools (e.g., Brooks, Terrace) documenting American shows--are complemented by many, sometimes rare, photo stills. A potentially useful tool for Americans in that many of these programs have been broadcast here on PBS, independent TV channels, or cable networks (e.g., A & E).

Individual Programs

--*The Addams Family*

Cox, Stephen, and John Astin. The Addams Chronicles: An Altogether Ooky Look at the Addams Family. Cumberland House, 1998. 2nd ed., rev & enlarged. 240p. il. $20.95. ISBN 1888952911.
The source provides a wealth of information about the zany characters created by magazine illustrator Charles Addams and the television show which turned them into household words. Behind-the-scenes stories and exclusive interviews with cast members and the program's creator are complemented by a wide array of previously unpublished pictures (most in black and white). The failure to cover the Hollywood films (starring the late Raul Julia) and 1990s television show beyond a passing reference represents the work's most notable flaw.

--*Ally McBeal*

Mitchell, Kathy. Ally McBeal: The Totally Unauthorized Guide. Boston: Little, Brown, 1998. 192p. il. $12.99 pap. ISBN 0446675326.
This unauthorized guide takes an irreverent, light- hearted approach to the hit sitcom. In addition to a wealth of factual trivia, Mitchell attempts to surmise what goes on inside

McBeal's head. Includes a concise episode guide which includes a critique of each show by the author.

--*American Bandstand*

Clark, Dick, and Fred Bronson. Dick Clark's American Bandstand. New York: HarperCollins, 1997. il. $20.00 pap. ISBN 0067574564.
Relates the story of the program's rise from a local Philadelphia dance program to national prominence as an icon of the rock 'n' roll youth subculture. Clark's behind-the-scene commentary--including anecdotes about performers and sidebars offering facts about the music and notable dancers participating on the show--is enhanced by copiously captioned photographs (more than 250 in all) from the Bandstand archives.

--*The Andy Griffith Show*

Beck, Ken, and Jim Clark. The Andy Griffith Show Book: From Miracle Salve to Kerosene Cucumbers; The Complete Guide to One of Television's Best-Loved Shows. Designed by Paolo Pepe. 35th ed. New York: St. Martin's Press, 1995. 219p. il. $13.95 pap. ISBN 0312117418.
The continued revision of this companion owes much to the continued popularity of *The Andy Griffith Show* through syndication. Strengths include the abundance of cast photos (including a color photo insert) and the Introduction's insightful assessment of the program.

Robinson, Dale, and David Fernandes. The Definitive Andy Griffith Show Reference: Episode -by-Episode, with Cast and Production Biographies and a Guide to Collectibles. Introduction by Andy Lore. Jefferson, NC: McFarland, 1996. 336p. $45.00. ISBN 0786401362.
This source effectively combines a number of approaches; i.e., an inventory of series episodes (with synopses), concise bios of cast members and key production personnel, and merchandise price guide.

Spignesi, Stephen. Mayberry, My Hometown: The Ultimate Guidebook to America's Favorite TV Small Town. Ann Arbor, MI: Popular Culture, Ink, 1991. 300p. il., index. $19.95 pap.
Mayberry, My Hometown represents the best of all worlds for a reference tool: while notable for its thoroughgoing attention to detail and abundance of cross-references, it also is an entertaining cornucopia of information regarding *The Andy Griffith Show*, and two spin-off series, *Gomer Pyle, U.S.M.C.* and *Mayberry, R.F.D.* The book includes the following sections: Part I - The Mayberry Pocket Almanac: A Handy Guide to Mayberry People, Places & Things (including floor plans, time slots and Nielsen Rankings by season, character frequency charts, etc.); Part II - The Mayberry Encyclopedia: From "A1A" to "Zone Detection System"; Part III - Going Home to Mayberry: A Look at the "Return"; Part IV - Mayberry Confidential: Some of Our Favorite Mayberryites Speak Their Minds; Part V - Mayberry Fandom: "A Rendezvous With Destiny"; and Part VI - The Subconscious Prober Primer: A Topical Index to the Encyclopedia. The text is

complemented by black-and-white photos and sidebar essays (e.g., Richard Kelly's "Staying Alive in Mayberry," which delineates the universal qualities of that universe). The work has its faults, most notably the failure to arrange episodes chronologically (Spignesi instead lists them alphabetically by obscure program titles) and the terseness of plot summaries (often just a sentence or two in length).

--As the World Turns

Poll, Julie. As the World Turns: The Complete Family Scrapbook; Special 40th Anniversary Edition. Introduction by Helen Wagner. Genl Publishing Group, 1998. 304p. il. $14.95 pap. ISBN 1575441101.
Poll, with the complete support of Procter & Gamble Productions, has assembled a nostalgic overview of this soap opera universe based in the fictional town of Oakdale. The text--which covers factors at the core of the program's immense popularity, notable plot twists, and key cast members--is enhanced by some 200 photographs (generally promotional shots and stills from actual episodes).

--The Avengers

Carraze, Alain, Jean-Luc Putheaud, and Alex J. Geairns. The Avengers Companion. BB&T, 1998. 196p. il. $19.95 pap. ISBN 0912333618.
The source provides information on all facets of the classic 1960s series, including its history, episode breakdown, and cast credits. Also covers the Warner Brothers feature film, *The Avengers* (1998), starring Ama Thurman and Sean Connery. Lavishly illustrated with 250 photos, 112 of which are in color.

Rogers, Dave. The Complete Avengers: Everything You Ever Waned to Know About the Avengers and the New Avengers. Griffin, 1998. 285p. il. $14.95 pap. ISBN 0312031874.
Although many reference tools delineating this British program are currently available--including *The Avengers Dossier*, by Paul Cornell et al, *The Avengers and Me*, by Patrick Macnee and Dave Rogers, and *The Avengers: Too Many Targets*, by John Peel and Dave Rogers--this is most comprehensively researched of the lot. It offers a general overview, detailed episode-by-episode descriptions, and background information on the leading actors or characters. The text is supplemented by an in-depth memorabilia listing for collectors and over 200 lavish photographs.

--Babylon 5

Bassom, David. The A-Z Guide to Babylon 5. Dell, 1997. 448p. $6.99 pap. ISBN 0440223857.
Encyclopedic compendium of the award-winning, sci- fi hit program, covering everything from characters to concept. The prime flaws are poor production, an awkward size (0.91 x 4.21 x 6.90 inches), and limitation of coverage to the first two seasons.

--The Beverly Hillbillies

Cox, Stephen. The Beverly Hillbillies. Foreword by Buddy Ebsen. New
York: Harper Perennial/Harper Collins, 1993. 243p. il. ISBN 0-06-097565-2 (pbk.)
A substantial portion of the work is devoted to a historical survey of the program
along with concise biographies of the leading cast members. The text is complemented
by the liberal use of sidebars (e.g., "Hillbillies on Parade," covering the show's notable
merchandising tie- ins) and black-and-white photos from both on and off the set. Also
includes the "Episode Guide," a chronological inventory of all broadcast installments of
the program (106 in black and white, 168 in color), and "Afterword," an essay on the
parodies inspired by the theme song, "The Ballad of Jed Clampett."

--Bonanza

Shapiro, Melany. Bonanza: The Definitive Ponderosa Companion. Cyclone, 1997.
176p. il. index of guest stars. $19.95 pap. ISBN 1890723185.
Shapiro analyzes the forces behind the program's unprecedented success; i.e., number
one Nielsen rating for a substantial portion of its ten-year run with a peak audience of 480
million viewers in 97 countries. Includes episode summaries, biographies of major cast
and supporting actors, writing and production credits, and a guided tour of the real- life
Ponderosa.

--The Brady Bunch

Moran, Elizabeth. Bradymania!: Everything You Always Wanted to Know--and a
Few Things You Probably Didn't. Adams Media Corporation, 1994. 239p. il. $9.95
pap. ISBN 1558504184.
Presents a cornucopia of information relating to the evolution of the program,
individual episodes, updated cast biographies, the first Paramount feature film released in
late 1994, etc. The abundance of photos--many of which have not been previously
published--contributes to the nostalgic scrapbook feel of the work.

--Buffy the Vampire Slayer

Gence, Ngaire E. The Buffy Chronicles: The Unofficial Guide to Buffy the
Vampire Slayer. Three Rivers Press, 1998. 256p. black-and-white il. $15.00. ISBN
0609803425.
The work provides a wealth of details about the first season and a half of the series,
including episode descriptions, cast information, plot synopses, bloopers, behind-the-
scenes trivia, and sidebars such as "The Death Toll," a roster of who's been killed by
whom in each episode, and "I Fall to Pieces," a roadmap to the alternative music and
bands that make up the soundtrack. Well researched and lucidly written. The presence
of considerable outside material--e.g., a history of vampire legends, old b & w movie
stills, a retrospective of the Hollywood film that sparked interest in a TV series, a
discussion of the folklore behind the various creatures appearing in the various
episodes—could well represent the most controversial aspect of *The Buffy Chronicles*.

Golden, Christopher, Nancy Holder, and Keith R.A. Decandido. Buffy the Vampire Slayer: The Watcher's Guide. New York: Pocket Books, 1998. 298p. il. $14.00. ISBN 0671024337.
This official companion volume incorporates interviews, exclusive photos, a day on the set journal, plot summaries, a "Pop-Culture IQ" guide, factual pop- up balloons, a catalog of "Buffy's Bag of Tricks" (e.g., her weapns, spells, chants, incantations). Covers the first two years of the series.

--CNN

Flournoy, Don M., Jimmy Carter, and Robert K. Stewart. CNN; Making News in the Global Market. Champagne, IL: University of Illinois Press, 1999. 230p. $24.00 pap. ISBN 1960205429.
Profile of the cable network responsible for revolutionizing the mode of presenting television news. The work examines at length the impact CNN has had upon culture worldwide.

--*The Dukes of Hazzard*

Hofstede, David, and Catherine Bach. The Dukes of Hazzard: The Unofficial Companion. Renaissance, 1998. 272p. il. $14.95 pap. ISBN 1580630383.
A comprehensive, well written guide to the series. Includes an in-depth review of each episode spanning all seven seasons (1970-1985), biographical coverage of the cast members, behind-the-scenes anecdotes, fan club data, and a listing of merchandising tie-ins.
Also covers "Enos" and "The Dukes" cartoon series.

--*ESPN's Sport Center*

Olberman, Keith, with Dan Patrick. The Big Show: Inside ESPN's Sports Center. Introduction by Bob Costas. New York: Pocket Books, 1997. 308p. il. $23.00. ISBN 0671009184. Also adapted, in truncated form, as an audio book.
A humorous look at the most popular program on the largest cable network in the United States. Olberman and Patrick address both the series and the sports world (e.g., the greatest athletes of all time, on-the-air errors, problems inherent in the baseball all of fame selection process). Chapters include"Bill Buckner--What Happened?," "How to Be a Sportscaster When You Grow Up," and "Put Your Baseball Cards in Yo ur Bicycle Spokes, Now!"

--*Fawlty Towers*

Cleese, John, with Connie Booth. Complete Fawlty Towers. New York: Pantheon Books, 1989. 333p. il. $16.00 pap. ISBN 0679721274.
Provides the complete and unexpurgated scripts of the original British comedy series, twelve episodes in all. While many Americans are already familiar with the mid-1970s

program via videotape and DVD releases as well as endless PBS reruns, they will undoubtedly find a close-up look at the screenplays--complemented by photo stills--an avenue for further insight and mirth.

--Friends

Wild, David. Friends: The Official Companion. Main Street Books, 1995. il. $12.95 pap. ISBN 0385483295.
With *Friends* now in syndication, this guide provides a wide array of information about the program. It includes plot summaries of the first season, snippets of dialogue, interviews with the cast, more than 100 photos (many not previously available), a quiz, an "Uncensored Tail- All" by Marcel the monkey, and a wealth of trivia.
Hogan's Heroes.

Royce, Brenda Scott. Hogan's Heroes: A Comprehensive Reference to the 1965-1971 Television Comedy Series, with Cast Biographies and an Episode Guide. Jefferson, NC: McFarland, 1993. 296p. bibl., index. $39.95. ISBN 0899507964.
Provides a multi- faceted overview of the program, from conception to cancellation following the sixth season. In addition to separate biographies for all key cast members and a season-by-season episode breakdown, the work covers ratings, awards, promotion, language considerations, costumes and signature props, and supplementary personnel (e.g., stock players, directors, writers).

--I Love Lucy

Andrews, Bart. The "I Love Lucy" Book. Foreword by Jess Oppenheimer. Garden City, NY: Dolphin/Doubleday, 1985. 423p. il., index. $11.95 pap. ISBN 0-385-1903-6.
A revised edition of the author's *Lucy & Ricky & Fred & Ethel* (1976), the work is equally divided into a history of the program (including a survey of Lucille Ball's show business career) and an "I Love Lucy" Log, a chronologically arranged listing of episodes. Log entries include date of original broadcast, date filmed, rating/audience share, supporting cast, music selections, and plot summary. The abundance of black-and-white photographs (program stills, fanzine reproductions, publicity shots, etc.) were culled from Viacom and Andrews' personal collection. Accessibility is greatly enhanced by the Handy-Dandy Episode Finder, a key word index referring the user to the appropriate episode number. Includes a Foreword by Jess Oppenheimer, producer of the program during its early years.

--Jeopardy!

Eisenberg, Harry. Jeopardy!: A Revealing Look Inside TV's Top Quiz Show; Contestants and Question Selection Process Unveiled. Lifetime Books, 1995. $18.95 pap. ed. il. ISBN 0811908062.
Eisenberg, the program's former editorial associate producer, provides an insider's view of *JEOPARDY!* including how contestants are chosen, how categories are selected, how questions are created, how host Alex Trebek once threatened to quit, the

development of the show and its staffing, and countless other secrets. In addition, the tool offers pointers regarding how to get on the program--and win.

--*Leave It to Beaver*

Mathers, Jerry, with Herb Fagen. And Jerry Mathers As "the Beaver." Boulevard, 1998. 272p. il. $14.00 pap. ISBN 0425163709.
In essence, an autobiography; Mathers covers his personal life as well as challenges beyond his famous role as Theodore "Beaver" Cleaver. Also includes ample *Leave It to Beaver* trivia; e.g., his most embarrassing moments on the set, his relationships with cast members).

--*M.A.S.H.*

Kalter, Suzy. The Complete Book of M*A*S*H. Abradale Press, 1988. Il. $19.98. ISBN 0810980835.
Provides an overview of the highly successful comedy series, which ran for eleven seasons in the 1970s and early 1980s. Includes synopses of each of the 251 episodes and interviews with the program's actors and production staff. Over 200 photographs illustrate memorable scenes and backstage activities. The omission of the subplots of each episode represent the book's only notable weakness.
M.T.V.

Goodwin, Andrew. Dancing in the Distraction Factory: Music Television and Popular Culture. Minneapolis: University of Minnesota Press, 1992. 237p. il. $18.95 pap. ISBN 0816620636. Also available in hardcover edition.

--*The Prisoner*

Carraze, Alain, and Helene Oswald. The Prisoner: A Televisionary Masterpiece. Christine Donougher, translater. London Bridge, 1996. 241p. 241p. il. ISBN 0863695574.
Provides comprehensive reviews of all seventeen episodes of the late 1960s British drama as well as analytical essays from guest commentators such as Isaac Asimov. The text is complemented by the lavish use of photos from each episode (plus production pictures) and an interview with Patrick McGoohan.

--*Seinfeld*

Gattuso, Greg. Seinfeld Universe: The Entire Domain. Carol Publishing Group, 1998. 198p. il. $12.00 pap. ISBN 0806520019.
The source includes historical background, profiles the real- life personalities who provided the inspiration for the TV characters, and tours New York locations immortalized by the program. Gattuso's credentials include editing and publishing "Nothing: The Newsletter for Seinfeld Fans."

Seinfeld, Jerry. The Seinfeld Scripts: The First and Second Seasons. New York: HarperCollins, 1998. 608p. $17.95 pap. ISBN 0060953039.
The uniform excellence of the writing in *Seinfeld* renders its scripts required reading for fans of the program and sitcoms in general. Includes the complete scripts from the first two seasons of the show, seventeen episodes overall.

--Star Trek

Andreadis, Athena. To Seek Out New Life; The Biology of Star Trek. New York: Crown, 1999. 288p. il. $12.00 pap. ISBN 0609804219.

Greenwald, Jeff. Future Perfect: How Star Trek Conquered Planet Earth. New York: Viking, 1998. 256p. $23.95. ISBN 0670873993.
A product of the author's exhaustive search for the sociological impact of the series, the book combines a historical survey with insights gleaned from the activities of fan clubs worldwide, interviews with celebrities (e.g., the Dalai Lama, Kurt Vonnegut Jr., Arthur C. Clarke, Leonard Nimoy) and various subject experts, and assorted documentation. The text is complemented by a multitude of sidebars providing additional perspectives on the show; e.g., "filk song" lyrics (substituting Trek themes for the words of popular songs), a black woman astronaut deriving inspiratio n from Lt. Uhura, the program title in a number of foreign languages.

Lundeen, Jan, and Jon G. Wagner. Deep Space and Sacred Time: Star Trek in the American Mythos. Praeger, 1998. 280p. $27.95. ISBN 0275962253.
Lundeen, a nursing teacher at Carl Sandburg College, and Wagner, a Professor of Anthropology at Knox College, argue that *Star Trek* functions as a secular humanist mythology for many Americans in its exploration and mediation of the ambiguities of modern culture while communicating hope and empowerment in an orderly cosmos. The program's poetics of religion, gender, progress, and human difference have evolved to meet the changing demands of liberal doctrine from the Vietnam era to the age of postmodern cynicism.

Okuda, Michael, and Denise Okuda. Star Trek: Chronology. New York: Pocket Books, 1996, c1993. revised and updated edition. Il. $25.00 pap. ISBN 0671536109.
Delineates episodes from the original 1960s series (three years), *Star Trek: The Next Generation* (seven years), *Deep Space Nine* (four years), and *Star Trek: Voyager* (two years) in addition to the related feature films. The text is augmented by more than 1,000 color photos and exhaustive appendixes on the individual series, characters, science and technology tie- ins, alternate timelines, and episode writing credits.

--Three's Company

Mann, Chris. Come and Knock on Our Door: A Hers and Hers and His Guide to "Three's Company." Foreword by Joyce DeWitt. New York: St. Martin's, 1998. 289p. il. $17.95 pap. ISBN 0312168039.

Mann combines biographies of cast members, interviews (with over sixty actors, producers, directors, and crew members), and general analysis in dissecting one of the best known sitcoms of the 1970s. The book's behind-the-scenes insights reveal that personal, financial, and creative conflicts threatened to undermine the outward success of the program. Includes commentaries on each episode.

--TV Nation

Moore, Michael, and Kathleen R. Glynn. Adventures in a TV Nation. New York: HarperCollins, 1998. 288p. $13.00 pap. ISBN 0060988096.
An insider's look at the controversial, Emmy Award-winning NBC series. Covers both the most popular segments and those not allowed on the air. The appendixes include The TV Nation Polls, The Shows (an inventory of episodes), How to Get Stuff, and TV Nation Resources.

--The Twilight Zone

Zicree, Marc Scott. The Twilight Zone Companion. 2nd ed. Silman Jam, 1992. 466p. il. $15.95 pap. ISBN 1879505096.
An update of the 1983 American Book Award nominee, *The Twilight Zone Companion* is, first and foremost, an episode guidebook. Each entry incorporates a plot synopsis, narration by show creator Rod Serling, critical commentary, behind-the-scenes anecdotes from the original artist for the series, and an exhaustive list of cast and credits. The source also includes Zicree's overview of the program from inception to cancellation as well as syndication and ensuing offshoots and remakes. The text is enhanced by more than 200 production photos.

--Twin Peaks

Lavery, David, ed. Full of Secrets: Critical Approaches to Twin Peaks. Detroit: Wayne State University Press, 1995. 281p. $19.95 pap. (Contemporary Film and Television) ISBN 0814325068.
Academic in tone, the work includes analytical essays and supplementary data such as a scene breakdown of each episode, a calendar of red- letter dates relating to plot development, and lists of cast members, directors, and writers for each episode. The essays cover the art and politics of the show, its use of music, a feminist interpretation of plotting and character development, and postmodernism and television.

--The X-Files

Carter, Chris. The Art of the X-Files. Introduction by William Gibson. New York: Harper Prism, 1998. 156p. il. $35.00 ISBN 0061050377.
Built around 75 paintings, photos, sculptures, graphic and digital media creations, the book attempts to evoke the dark, edgy vision of *The X-Files*. Many of the selections are accompanied by a statement from the artist, expounding on the sources of inspiration, including episodes, a line of dialogue, a particular incident, and overall series themes.

Farrand, Phil. The Nitpicker's Guide for X-Files. Dell, 1997. 416p. il. $12.95. ISBN 0440508088.

Part of a successful line of unauthorized fact-books devoted to popular TV shows, *The Nitpicker's Guide for X-Files* includes reveiws of every episode for the first four seasons, elaboration on conspiracy theories, trivia questions and interesting facts, changed premises, equipment flubs, plot oversights, online interviews, and web site data. Widely considered to be the best of some two dozen reference tools devoted to this sci- fi hit (see amazon.com); others of note include *The Unauthorized X-Cyclopedia*, by James Hatfield and George Burt; *I Want to Believe: the Official Guide to the X-Files*, by Andy Meisler, et al.; and *What's Your X-Files' I.Q.?* by Marc Shapiro.

Lavery, David, Angela Hague, and Marla Cartwright, editors. Deny All Knowledge: Reading the X-Files. Syracuse, NY: Syracuse University Press, 1996. 280p. $49.95. ISBN 0815627173. Also available in paperback edition.

While overly burdened with metaphors and overblown interpretations in a series of essays largely written by university graduate students, the insights found here represent an anecdote to the trivial details comprising the majority of works of this ilk. Topics covered include the Mulder/Scully relationship, the program's online fan base, and gender liminality.

Mangels, Andy. Beyond Mulder and Scully: The Mysterious Characters of "The X-Files." New York: Citadel, 1998. 256p. il. $16.95. ISBN 0806519339.

Provides facts about the supporting characters--and actors who play them--appearing on the popular TV sci- fi series, including "Deep Throat," "X," and "Cigarette Smoking Man." The information is imparted in breezy fashion via biographies, interviews, and trivia sidebars.

INDEXES--FILM INDUSTRY

Alvarez, Max Joseph. Index to Motion Pictures Reviewed by Variety, 1907-1980. Metuchen, NJ: Scarecrow Press, 1982. 520p. $32.50. ISBN 0-8108-1515-X.

All motion pictures, features and shorts, reviewed by the trade paper *Variety* are catalogued in this exceptionally fine research tool. Titles are given in alphabetical order followed by the review date and page number. A must for all film researchers.

Perry, Jeb H. Variety Obits: An Index to Obituaries in Variety, 1905-1978. Metuchen, NJ: Scarecrow Press, 1980. 322p. $16.00. ISBN 0-1808-1289-4.

As the title implies, this book serves as an index to death notices in the show business trade paper *Variety*. Some

15,000 names are included with age, death date, profession, date of publication and page number. This volume should be highly useful to researchers.

Spechr, Paul C. with Gunnar Lundquist. American Film Personnel and Company Credits, 1908-1920: Filmographies Recorded by Authoritative Organizational and Personal Names From Lauritzen and Lundquist's American Film-Index. Jefferson, NC: McFarland, 1996. 718p. $110.00. ISBN 0-7864-0255-5.
Einar Lauritzen and Gunnar Lundquist's groundbreaking Volumes, *American Film-Index, 1908-1915* (1976) and *American Film-Index, 1916-1920* (1984), together listed credits for more than 33,000 American movies. Unfortunately these books were not indexed in the traditional sense and this volume corrects that oversight by indexing them by production companies and personal names. In compiling filmographies, this book stands by itself as a useful reference source, but its importance to the chronicling of film history is best shown when it is used in tandem with the two base volumes. The book, however, represents a major contribution to cinema research.

Abstracts/Critiques/Reviews

Brode, Douglas. Lost Films of the Fifties. Secaucus, NJ: Citadel Press, 1991. 287p. $15.95 pap. ISBN 0-8065-1092-7. Useful critiques of dozens of lesser covered feature films from the 1950s with cast, credits, plots. Among the titles included are *The Woman of Pier 13* (1950), *Five* (1951), *Breaking the Sound Barrier* (1952), *Split Second* (1952), *The Egyptian* (1954), *Battle Cry* (1955), *Helen of Troy* (!956), *1984* (1956), *Jeanne Eagles* (!957), *The Witches of Salem* (1958), and *The Mouse That Roared* (!959).

Elley, Derek. Variety Movie Guide. New York: Prentice Hall, 1992. 704p. $20.00 pap. ISBN 0-13-928342-0. Here are condensed *Variety* reviews for more tha n 5,000 feature films, from 1914 to the early 1990. Brief cast and credits are given in addition to the reviews, making this a useful tool, although no substitute for the entire set of reviews which is also available.

Garbicz, Adam, and Jacek Klinowski. Cinema, The Magic Vehicle: A Guide to Its Achievement, Journey Two: The Cinema in the Fifties. Metuchen, NJ: Scarecrow Press, 1979. 551p. $25.00. ISBN 0-8108-1241-X.

Literate discussion of over 300 feature films from around the world released in the 1950s, with cast, credits, plots, and critiques. Movies from the Italian Neorealism, New Soviet Cinema, Polish School, and French Nouvelle Vague are included as are the works of acclaimed directors like Robert Bresson, Ingmar Bergman, Federico Fellini, and Alfred Hitchcock. Preceded by the same authors' *Cinema, The Magic Vehicle: A Guide To Its Achievement, Journey One: The Cinema Through 1949* (Metuchen, NJ: Scarecrow Press, 1975. 551p. $20.50. ISBN 0-8108-0801-3.

Herx, Henry, and Zaza, Tony. The Family Guide to Movies On. New York: Crossroad, 1988. 331p. ISBN 0-8245-0816-5.
Compiled by managers of the United States Catholic Conference's Department of Communciations' media review and educational services, this useful reference work gives thumbnail reviews of over 5,000 feature films available on video. The book is designed to aid parents on the moral suitability of movies in their selection of videos and also attempts to check the films entertainment value.

Huffhines, Kathy Schulz, ed. Foreign Affairs: The National Society of Film Critics' Video Guide to Foreign Films. San Francisco: Mercury House, 1991. 568p. $14.95 pap. ISBN 1-56279-016-1.
Dozens of foreign films from the 1920s through the 1980s are reviewed in brief essays by a number of writers in this worthwhile volume. The 300 films included in the text are available for viewing at video stores, etc., thus making the book more valuable for fans of foreign films.

The Phantom's Ultimate Video Guide. New York: Dell, 1989. 756p. il. $12.95 pap. ISBN 0440-50212-8.
The Phantom of the Movies reviews over 4,000 action, cult, horror and science fiction films in this fun to read oversized softbound volume. In addition, the book contains biography sidebars, plenty of photos, and sections on movie serials and TV favorites on video.

Salem, James M. A Guide to Critical Reviews, Part IV: The Screenplay, Supplement One: 1963-1980. Metuchen, NJ: Scarecrow 1982. 708p. $65.00. ISBN 0-8108-1553-2.
Useful research tool which lists source reviews for hundreds of feature films released between 1963 and 1980. Preceded by *A Guide to Critical Reviews: American Drama,*

1900- (1973), A Guide to Critical Reviews: The Musical, 1909- (1976), A Guide to Critical Reviews: The Screenplay from 'The Jazz Singer' and "Dr. Strangelove" (2 volumes, 1971), and *A Guide to Critical Reviews: Foreign Drama, 1909-1977*, published by Scarecrow Press.

Slide, Anthony, and Wagenknecht, Edward. Fifty Great American Silent Films 1912-1920: A Pictorial Survey. New York: Dover, 1980. 140p. il. $6.95 pap. ISBN 0-486-23985-3.
Although it does contain many interesting photographs, this "Pictorial Survey" is a fine accounting of fifty early silent feature films. Provided are cast and credits, plot synopsis and lucid commentary on the individual films by its authors, two top authorities on silent movies. Among the movies included are *From the Manger to the Cross, The Spoilers, The Birth of a Nation, A Daughter of the Gods, A Tale of Two Cities, Spirit of '76, Broken Blossoms, Anne of Green Gables*, and *The Penalty*.

Stanley, John. John Stanley's Creature Features Movie Guide Strikes Again. 4th ed. Pacifica, CA: Creatures at Large Press, 1994. 454p. il. $50.00. ISBN 0-940064-09-X.
Former San Francisco-Bay Area TV horror film host John Stanley continues his "Creature Feature" series with an updated volume giving capsule reviews of more than 5,600 horror, science fiction, and fantasy feature films. While Stanley's reviews are brief, they are also informative, providing film plot, release year, stars, director(s), and video sources. Sprinkled with illustrations, the book is informative although the author is quite opinionated. The volume's ma in asset consists of including movies often not found in other sources. On the other hand, many titles are included; however, the user is often referred to editions 1-3 (which may not be available) for in-depth information. Also available as a paperback.

Thompson, Frank. Lost Films: Important Movies That Disappeared. New York: Citadel Press, 1996. 298p. $16.95 pap. ISBN 0-8065-1604-6.
As noted by its title, this volume takes a look at important movies that are no longer extant. Twenty-seven Hollywood films from 1911 to 1929 are discussed with only one, *4 Devils* (1929), having a dialogue version; the rest being silents. In addition to cast, credits, and plot synopsis, the author provides in-depth commentary on each of the films included. Among them are *The Immortal Alamo* (1911), *Damaged Goods* (1914), *A Daughter of the Gods* (1916),

Cleopatra (1917), *The Miracle Man* (1919), *That Royale Girl* (1926), *Beau Sabreur* (1928), and *The Case of Lena Smith* (1929). An important work on films unjustly overlooked because they no longer exist.

Tyler, Parker. Classics of the Foreign Film: A Pictorial Treasury. New York: Citadel Press, 1962. 253p. il. $8.50. Landmark volume which discusses a number of foreign classic film in a lucid manner with appropriate illustrations. Among the titles included are *The Cabinet of Dr. Caligari* (1919), *Napoleon* (1925), *Metropolis* (!928), *Der Blaue Angel* (!930), *Que Viva Mexico* (1932), *The 39 Steps* (1935), *Day of Wrath* (1943), *Dead of Night* (1946), *Hamlet* (1948), *Rashomon* (1951), *La Strada* (1954), *Wild Strawberries* (1959), and *La Notte* (1961). A must for readers interested in foreign films.

Weldon, Michael J. The Psychotronic Video Guide. New York: St. Martin's/Griffin, 1996. il. $29.95 pap. ISBN 0-312-13149-6.
A follow- up to the above book, this volume is mainly made up of reviews which appeared in the author's *Psychotronic Video* magazine. Like the initial work, this one provides fun reading in its reviews of several thousand offbeat movies as well as the inclusion of 450-odd illustrations. This volume is especially useful for researchers in that it contains information on films not generally included in other sources.

Zinman, David. 50 Classic Motion Pictures. New York: Chelsea House, 1983. 311p. il. $24.95. ISBN 0-87754-3747.
Originally published in 1970, the work provided thorough coverage of fifty notable sound films of the 1930s and 1940s. Now including representation of more recent films, it is organized under umbrella titles such ad stars, genres, and directors.

INDEXES--TELEVISION

Moulds, Michael, ed. International Index to Television Periodicals: an Annotated Guide, 1979/80- . London: International Federation of Film Archives [1983]- . biennial. author index.
A selective index--reflecting worldwide literature of critical or aesthetic value--of approximately 100 media journals. The concise annotations address the scope and/or content of each article. Divided into the following sections: general subjects, individual programs and TV films, and biography. Also available in electronic form as *International Filmarchive CD-ROM* (London: FIAF, 1993?- . semiannual).

Prouty, Howard H., ed. Variety Television Reviews, 1923-1988. 15 volumes. New York: Garland, 1989-1991. indexes. $80.00 ea.; except Volume 18 (1993-1994), $200.00. ISBN 0-8240-2587-3 (vol. 1).
A chronologically arranged compilation of reprinted television reviews appearing in the leading entertainment trade tabloid, *Variety*. Accessibility is enhanced by title, subject, name, local programming, and international programming indexes. The tool is continued by *Variety and Daily Variety Television Reviews*, Volume 16 [1989/90]- , Garland, 1992- , biennial.

Transcript/Video Index, 1992: A Comprehensive Guide to Television and Radio News and Public Affairs Programming. Volume 5: Number 13. 2 volumes. Denver, CO: Journal Graphics, 1993. $49.95 pap./set. ISBN 1-879-762-06-4.
Expanded from the one-volume coverage of 1991, this edition incorporates 125 programs, the majority of which are television broadcasts. The materials are arranged under broad subject headings along with a small number of name headings for notable personalities. Entries include program title, an abstract, and transcript cost. While larger libraries possess the means to obtain information on Journal Graphics transcriptions via Mead Data's LEXIS/NEXIS online service, this tool provides access to many news and "tabloid television" transcripts not available electronically. Includes sections on transcript sets available on various topics and videocassettes which can be privately purchased.

JOURNALS--GENERAL

Audio-Visual Communications. 1961-. Monthly. Mike Yuhas, ed. Media Horizons, Inc., 50 W. 23rd St., New York, NY 10010-5292. il., adv., rev.
The publication concentrates on the uses of media in business, advertising, and promotion, including product reviews and listings as well as news on corporate developments, awards announcements, and the analysis of general media trends.

Broadcasting: The Fifth Estate. 1931-. Weekly. Lawrence B. Taishoff, ed. Broadcasting Publications, 1735 DeSales St., NW, Washington, D.C. 20036. il., adv., rev.
A leading industry trade publication, it encompasses radio, television, cable, satellite, home video, and the allied arts in covering new technological developments, relevant legislation, FCC regulations, and market and personnel news.

JOURNALS--FILM INDUSTRY

American Film: The Magazine of the Film and Television Arts. 1975-. 10/yr. Susan Linfield, ed. American Film Institute, M.D. Publications, Inc., 3 E. 54th St., New York, NY 10022. il., rev.
The highly readable artic les focus on contemporary films and television, with a particular emphasis on the Hollywood scene. Features are complemented by interviews,

seminars, editorials, and news notes covering both social and technical features of these media.

Cinefantastique. 1970-. 5/yr. Frederick S. Clarke, ed. P.O. Box 270, Oak Park, IL 60303. il., adv., film rev.
In its analysis of horror, fantasy, and science fiction films, this lavishly illustrated magazine touches upon thematic, aesthetic, financial, and technical considerations.

Classic Images. 1962-. Monthly. Bob King, ed. Lee Enterprises, Inc., 301 E. Third St., Muscatine, Iowa 52761. Il., adv., rev.
Samuel K. Rubin started this publication as the *8mm Collector* and it later expanded into *Classic Film Collector*. The tabloid size periodical features a potpourri of nostalgia and film history articles along with book reviews, interviews, current events, and advertisements. These is also a companion publication, *Films of the Golden Age*.

Cult Movies. 1993-. Michael Copner, ed. 6201 Sunset Blvd., Suite 152, Hollywood, CA 90028. Il., adv., film rev.
Advertised as "We Remember Forgetten Filkms," this nostalgia magazine leans to articles on horror, science fiction, and comedy films. It also emphasizes career studies, interviews, and reviews of movies of the past. While the publications often includes interesting material this is often offset by small print and newsprint paper with poor picture reproduction.

Film Comment. 1954-. 6/yr. Richard T. Jameson, ed. Film Society of Lincoln Center, 70 Lincoln Center Plaza, New York, NY 10023. Il., film rev., adv.
Slick bi-monthly magazine which features in-depth articles and reviews, primarily concerned with current cinema.

Film History. 1987-. Quarterly. Richard Koszarski, ed. Taylor & Francis, Inc., 242 Cherry St., Philadelphia, PA 19106. il.
The wide-ranging articles cover "the historical development of the motion picture, and [its] social, technological, and economic context." Included are profiles of relevant archives as well as reports of current publications, conferences, and research in progress.

Film Quarterly. 945-. Quarterly. Ernest Callenbach, ed. University of California Press, Berkeley, CA 94720. il., index, adv., rev.
The scholarly articles concentrate on the social and cultural elements of the film industry. The straightforward writing employed here should appeal to a lay audience in addition to academics.

Films in Review. 1949-. 10/yr. National Film Board of Review of Motion Pictures. il., rev.
The grand-daddy of all film history magazines, this small glossy-stock publication has featured a treasure trove of articles, career studies, and movie reviews in its half-century existence. While still a major force in the film history field, its heyday came in the 1950s and 1960s under the editorship of Henry Hart.

Filmfax. 1985-. 6/yr. Michael Stein and Sharon Lind Williams, eds. 10421/2
Michigan, Evanston, IL 60202. il., adv., rev.
Billed as "The Magazine of Unusual Film and Television," it includes in-depth
coverage of nostalgia movies and television shows along with interviews, book
and video reviews, and the liberal use of photographs.

Premiere. 1987-. 12/yr. James B. Meigs, ed. Hachette Filmpacchi Magazine II,
1633 Broadway, New York, NY 10019. il., adv., rev.
Calling itself "The Movie Magazine," this glossy-stock publication is mainly
comprised of articles and interviews dealing with contemporary cinema.

Psychotronic Video. 1985-. 4/yr. Michael J. Weldon, ed. 3309 Rt. 97,
Narrowsburg, NY 12764. il., adv., film rev.
Here is a magazine which covers movies falling outside the mainstream of
Hollywood releases. It includes in-depth interviews and career retrospectives,
film and video reviews, book and magazine reviews, a necrology, and letters
from readers.

Sight and Sound. 1990-. 12/yr. Philip Dodd, ed. British Film Institute, 21 Stephen
Street, London WIP 1PL, England. il., adv., film rev.
Incorporating the *Monthly Film Bulletin*, this publication represents a combination of
old and new cinema with comprehensive articles, reviews (films, videos, and books),
and news updates. The text also features an abundance of color photographs.

Video Watchdog. 1989-. 6/yr. Tim Lucas and Donna Lucas, editors. P.O. Box
5283, Cincinnati, OH 45205. il., film rev.
Aimed at fans of movies in the video format, this slick digest publication includes
indepth articles on films and filmmakers and reviews of videotapes, laser discs, DVDs,
CDs, and books. It attempts to keep readers abreast of current releases in addition to
providing regular updates on out-of-print videos.

Western Clippings. 1993-. 6/yr. Boyd Magers and Donna Magers, editors. 1312
Stagecoach Road, SE, Albuquerque, NM 87123. il., rev.
Concerned with western movies, the publication provides up-to-date information on
all aspects of the genre along with career studies, book and record reviews, current
happenings, and a lengthy necrology.

The World of Yesterday. Irregular. Ron Downey and Linda Downey, editors.
World of Yesterday Publications, 104 Chestnut Wood Drive, Waynesville, NC 28786.
il., adv., rev.
Nostalgia periodical whic h includes career articles, interviews, filmographies, and
reviews. It also has three associate publications: *Under Western Skies* (devoted to
cowboy movies), *The Films of Yesteryear*, and *The Golden Years of Radio & TV*.

JOURNALS--TELEVISION

Cablevision. 1975-. Semi- monthly. Craig Leddy, ed. Reed Elsevier Information, 825 Seventh Ave., New York, NY 10019. il. adv. ISSN 0361-8374.
The prestigious trade magazine offers feature articles on the cable television industry and related fields as well as departments on technological operations, marketing, programming, and pay-per-view. Each issue also documents the top 100 cable systems, network subscriber figures, and the top 100 multiple-system operators.

Satellite Orbit. 1982-. Monthly. Linda Casey, ed. CommTek Communications Corp., 8330 Boone Blvd., Suite 600, Vienna, VA 22182. il. adv. $57. ISSN 0732-7668.
Formerly titled, *Sat Guide*, the journal is comparable in scope and approach to *Satellite TV Week*. Includes a comprehensive satellite programming section with daily listings for almost 200 channels. The monthly programming department covers sports listings, shows by interest, satellite audio services, Ku-band channels, faces in the news, and pay-per-view breakdowns. Each issue also incorporates several general interest articles relating to satellite broadcast fare.

Satellite TV Week. 1981-. Weekly. James E. Scott, ed. Fortuna Communications Corp., 140 S. Fortuna Blvd., Fortuna, CA 95540-0308. il. adv. $59.95. ISSN 0744-7841.
Although it includes light articles on TV personalities and programs as well as departments concerned with industry news, letters from readers, lottery feeds, sports updates, and adult entertainment, day-to-day channel listings comprise the bulk of this publication. Issued in four editions, each covering a different U.S. time zone.

Television Index: The Network Program Production. 1949-. Weekly. BPI Communications, 1515 Broadway, 14th Floor, New York, NY 10036. index. ISSN 0739-5531.
A specialty newsletter that covers all new or rerun commercial network television series during a given week, the magazine also includes network specials, documentaries, and variety shows. The entries cite production credits, performers, advertisers, and historical background of the show. The publication package also includes the *TV Pro Log*--a source of up-to-date insider information regarding production news items, personnel developments, programs beginning production, etc.--and *Network Futures*, which provides calendar listings for upcoming television series, reruns, special shows, and notable scheduling modifications.

Television Quarterly: The Journal of the National Academy of Television Arts & Sciences. 1962-. Quarterly. Richard Pack, ed. National Academy of Television Arts & Sciences, 110 W. 57th St., New York, NY 10019. il. adv., rev. ISSN 0040-2796.
The publication's stated goal is to "deal with television's role in our complex society and its relationship to new technology." Major topics covered include programming, history of the medium, profiles of key figures, and contemporary issues. Its authors come from a wide array of backgrounds, most notably academia, freelance writers, and professionals from within the industry. Long considered the benchmark tool in the

literature on television, *Television Quarterly* can be appreciated by both experts and lay readers alike.

MANUALS--FILM INDUSTRY

Allen, Nancy. Film Study Collections: A Guide to Their Development and Use. New York: Frederick Ungar Publishing Company, 1979. 194p. $14.00. ISBN 0-8044-2011-7.
How to find and use material on film is outlined in this volume. Among its topics are building a basic film literature collection, unpublished scripts and non-print material as film study, periodical selection, cataloging and classifying material, stateside archives, film study libraries, and selected reference sources.

Sleeman, Phillip J., Bernard Queenan, and Francelia Butler. 200 Selected Film Classics for Children of All Ages: Where to Obtain Them and How to Use Them. Springfield, IL: Charles C. Thomas, 1984. 296p. il., index. ISBN 0-398-04869-X.
Focuses on films--available in English and the 16mm format-- derived from books of high literary quality that concentrate on "extending the life experiences of children and adults." The alphabetically arranged listing is supplemented by programming tips, a discussion of film rentals, a film care and projection guide, a directory of film companies and distributors, and an author index.

MANUALS--TELEVISION

Atchity, Kenneth J., and Chi-Li Wong. Writing Treatments That Sell: How to Create and Market Your Story Ideas to the Motion Picture and TV Industry. New York: Henry Holt, 1997. 256p. index. bibl. $14.95 pap. ISBN 0805042830.
Atchity and Wong, a couple of Hollywood writer-producers, have produced an engaging primer on developing an effective and salable treatment. The work covers such features as conflict, likable characters, plot twists, the climax, and visual drama. The content include The Nature and Role of the Treatment; Breaking into Television: Treatment for Television Movies; Treatments for Television Series; Treatments Based on True Stories; The Market for Treatments and What and How to Sell Them; Protecting Your Work; and Glossary and Entertainment Industry Terms.

Bare, Richard L. The Film Director: A Practical Guide to Motion Pictures and Television Techniques. Foreword by Robert Wise. New York: Macmillan, 1973. 243p. $15.00 pap. ISBN 002012130X.

Written by an award-winning TV and film director, the work looks at the basics of directing, ranging from the practice-based fundamentals of camera angle, sound synch, lighting, and setting to salary considerations (including typical compensation for reruns) and the methods of coaxing topnotch performances from actors and actresses. Provides firsthand examples from leading directors such as Alfred Hitchcock, Stanley Kubrick, George Stevens, and King Vidor.

Bender, Gary, and Michael Johnson. Call of the Game: What Really Goes On in the Broadcast Booth. Bonus Books, 1994. 263p. $19.95. ISBN 1566250137.
Bender, a TV sports announcer, provides a combination how-to and look-what-you're-getting-into overview relating to the coverage of sporting events. Geared to would-be broadcasters, the work touches upon both textbook theories and the more practical considerations of such a career (the latter is greatly enhanced through the inclusion of many personal anecdotes). Virtually all aspects of broadcasting are addressed; e.g., preparation for an on-air sports job, pre-event homework, play-by-play pointers, interacting with a booth partner and crew, handling controversy, developing a personal style.

Bension, Shmuel. The Producer's Masterguide , 1997/1998: The International Production Manual for Motion Picture, Television, Commercials, and Cable Industries. 17th ed. Producers Masterguide, 1997. $125.00 pap. ISBN 0935744169.
Widely considered a must for anymore wishing to pursue television work. It provides in-depth information for the U.S. and other major entertainment production nations.

Berland, Terry, and Deborah Ouellette. Breaking into Commercials: The Complete Guide to Marketing Yourself, Auditioning to Win, and Getting the Job. Introduction by Jason Alexander. Plume, 1997. 352p. $12.95 pap. ISBN 0452277701.
Berland, a veteran casting director, and Ouellette, an award-winning photographer/writer, combine to walk the reader through the commercial acting process, from resume preparation and getting head shots to residual and contract explanations. The authors many of the myths regarding success in this field; e.g., talent is the only quality that matters, you can pay to get on camera, all that is needed for voice-overs is a great demo tape. The text is augmented by question-and-answer interviews with over 75 industry experts and chapter-ending summaries.

Bernard, Ian, and Jack Lemmon. Film and Television Acting: From Stage to Screen. 2nd ed. Focal Press, 1997. 144p. $19.95 pap. ISBN 0240803019.
Offers guidelines on how to adapt one's prior training as an actor to film and TV sets. A new chapter by John Lithgow discusses the challenges faced by stage actors when they appear on a movie set for the first time.

Blacker, Irwin R. The Elements of Screenwriting: A Guide for Film and Television Writers. Reissue ed. New York: Macmillan, 1996. $9.95 pap. ISBN 002861450X.
Provides a comprehensive introduction to motion picture and TV screenwriting, from preliminary planning to the latter stages of the production process.

Block, Mervin. Writing Broadcast News: Shorter, Sharper, Stronger. rev. and expanded ed. Bonus Books, 1997. 310p. $29.95. ISBN 1566250846.
This informative introduction to the composition of broadcast news could be effectively employed as either a classroom text or reference sourcebook.

Blumenthal, Howard J., and Oliver R. Goodenough. This Business of Television. 2nd ed. 688p. il. $35.00. ISBN 0823077047. Includes computer disk compatible for both Windows and Macintosh.
The definitive reference source of its type, *The Business of Television* delineates the TV and video industries for producers, writers, broadcasters, executives, and other professionals. It also functions as an introductory guide for students and inexperienced staff. The data is organized into fifty chapters; three appendixes cover legal documents and forms, boilerplate contracts for the most common business business transactions, and a listing of industry contacts and addresses. Includes for following sections:
1) Distribution--networks and local stations, syndication, public television, cable systems and services, video formats, pay television, and new technologies (e.g., satellite delivery, high-definition TV); 2-3) FCC and other federal regulations, as well as legal concepts such as copyright, the right to privacy, libel and slander, and protection of society; 4) program production and financing; 5) audience measurement and advertising; 6) contract basics, legal entities, and tax issues; and 7) overview of television industries in other countries.

Boyd, Andrew. Broadcast Journalism: Techniques of Radio and TV News. 4th ed. Focal Press, 1997. 400p. $42.95 pap. ISBN 0240514653.
Provides guidelines regarding the basics of news writing, gathering and reading, interviewing, reporting, recording, editing, and scriptwriting. Also includes step-by-step instructions in the use of state-of-the-art broadcast equipment.

Brookbush, Virginia. Preproduction Planning for Video Taped Television. Community Television Agency, 1990. $10.00. ISBN 0961912006.
A straightforward introduction to the essentials of TV videotaping prior to the production stages.

Chambers, Everett. Producing TV Movies. E.C.P., Inc., 1993. $10.00 pap. ISBN 096205870X.
This industry insider's guide cover TV production from preproduction to postproduction, including tips on how to find a writer; create a script; sell a project; interact with networks, studios, and cast; edit; and handle a budget. Chambers has produced films for theatrical release and television, TV series (e.g., *Peyton Place, Airwolf, Colombo*), and commercials through North America and Europe.

Cooper, Dona. AFI Guide to Writing Great Screenplays for Film and TV. 2nd ed. Arco, 1998. 208p. $14.95. ISBN 0028615557.
Cooper, a television programming executive and former instructor at the American Film Institute Center for Advanced Film and Television Studies, guides the reader through the steps of the screenwriting process, including plot structuring, character

development, crafting the screenplay, and selling it to studios and producers. Rather than adhering to a list of arbitrary rules, the work provides a detailed analysis of how humans process story information. Aspiring writers are encouraged to apply their own take on story dynamics in developing a screenplay which effectively conveys the emotions they wish to elicit from an audience.

Cury, Ivan. Directing and Producing for Television: A Format Approach. Focal Press, 1998. 336p. $34.95 pap. ISBN 0240802810.
The work emphasizes the hands-on portion of the director's responsibilities in preproduction, production, and post production. Cury approaches these responsibilities by analyzing each format--panel shows, music programming, narrative forms, demonstrations, public service announcements, documentaries, news presentations, etc.--and related procedures. Noting that students tend to be proficient in the use of equipment while lacking in production technique, Cury addresses practical concerns such as what outlines are needed by whom and why, how to mark a script, and the features of an effective rehearsal agenda.

Delamar, Penny. The Complete Make -Up Artist: Working in Film, Television and Theatre. Evanston, IL: Northwestern University Press, 1995. $29.95 pap. ISBN 0810112582.
The basic approach should prove useful to novices, particularly the guidelines for obtaining professional training. Experienced professional make- up staff, however, will find fault with the shortage of information on film and television lighting and camera effects.

Dominick, Joseph R., and others. Broadcasting/Cable and Beyond: An Introduction to Mode rn Electronic Media. 3rd ed. New York: McGraw-Hill College Division, 1995. $57.00. ISBN 0070179883.
Surveys the broadcasting and career industries, including historical background, regulatory and economic aspects, and career opportunities. The third edition is not only fully revised and updated, but has incorporated new anecdotes and sidebars, coverage of the technologies central to the information superhighway, and chapter-opening "freezeframes" which highlight carious facts and figures likely to stimulate reader interest.

Eastman, Susan Tyler, with Douglas A. Ferguson. Broadcast/Cable Programming: Strategies and Practices. 5th ed. Wadsworth, 1996. 608p. $66.95 pap. ISBN 0534507441.
The authors discuss the electronic media programming process and the types of issues and strategies that are currently prominent in the field.

Fridell, Squire. Acting in Television Commercials for Fun and Profit. Barry Geller, illustrator. 3rd ed. New York: Crown, 1995. il. $15.00. ISBN 0517884372.
Fridell, an accomplished TV commercial actor (he has been featured in 17,000 commercials), provides inside pointers for breaking into and maintaining success within the commercial industry. This revision includes updated lists of agents, union offices,

and publications. The step-by-step instructions are tailored to beginners in the commercial acting business.

Graf, Rudolf F., with William Sheets. Video Scrambling & Descrambling for Satellite & Cable TV. Butterworth-Heinemann, 1997. 46p. $24.95 pap. ISBN 0750699450.
In addition to presenting the basics (e.g., theoretical background, circuitry schematics) of cable scrambling and descrambling, the reader can apply these principles effectively to many other electrical systems. However, the book may be too technical for use by the average electronics or computer buff.

Grant, August E. Broadcast Technology Update: Production and Transmission. Peter B. Seel, ed. Focal Press, 1997. 240p. $24.95 pap. ISBN 0240802845.
Provides a basic foundation to digital broadcast technology. Includes an associated web site which analyzes new technological developments appearing on the market since the book went to press.

Grant, Ruthie O. Show Biz Kids: How to Make Your Kid a Film, Television or Recording Star. Carrie See, photographer. 3rd ed. Etc Publishing House, 1997 344p. il. $16.95 pap. ISBN 0964133911.
The work provides straightforward guidelines to parents interested in preparing their children for a career in movies, television, or the music industry.

Grob, Bernard, and Charles Herndon. Basic Television and Video Systems. 6th ed. New York: Glencoe/McGraw-Hill, 1999. il. $15.00. ISBN 0028004388.
This work, consisting of an instruction manual and CD-ROM, provides an overview of TV and video fundamentals. An invaluable aid for individuals considering the purchase of video equipment.

Hart, John. The Art of the Storyboard: Storyboarding for Film, TV, and Animation. Butterworth-Heinemann, 1999. 224p. il. $29.95 pap. ISBN 024083299.
Hart, a portrait photographer and storyboard artist, surveys the historical development of this craft and analyzes the process of translating one's vision into a finished storyboard to be utilized by the cinematographer, set designer, special effects supervisor, and others. He utilizes his own storyboards--as well as those of other artists--to illustrate points in the text.

Hartwig, Robert L. Basic TV Technology: A Media Manual. 2nd ed. Focal Press, 1995. 172p. il $26.95 pap. ISBN 0240802284.
A practical guide to the operation of television equipment. The tool should prove useful to repair personnel and video hobbyists alike.

Hawthorne, Timothy R. The Complete Guide to Infomercial Marketing. NTC Business Books, 1997. $60.00 pap. ISBN 0844234451.
Provides practical step-by-step guidance regarding the production of infomercials. Hawthorne possesses impressive credentials within this field, having created some of the most successful infomercials ever during the past two decades.

Jarvis, Peter. The Essential TV Directors Handbook. Focal Press, 1998. 192p. $28.95 pap. ISBN 024051503X.
Outlines the basic operations relating to television direction and production. Geared to novices rather than personnel possessing a modicum of experience within this field.

Jurek, Ken. Careers in Video: Getting Ahead in Professional Television. Knowledge Industry Publications, 1989. 267p. $39.95 pap. ISBN 0867291699.
A no-nonsense introduction to a wide range of TV occupations, from technical operations to the performing and production arena. Jurek's guidelines have for-the-mostpart retained their utilitarian value, albeit with little mention of digital era resources.

Kruegle, Herman. CCTV Surveillance: Video Practices and Technology. Butterworth-Heinemann, 1996. $54.95 pap. ISBN 0750698365.
Documents the rise of closed circuit television technology as a distinct entity within the security industry. The work should prove useful to security managers, consultants, designers, dealers, installers, and others requiring practical information on when and how to use CCTV within the context of a security system.

Lee, Teresa A. Legal Research Guide to Television Broadcasting and Program Syndication. William & Hein & Co., 1995. 42p. $35.00. (Legal Research Guides, Volume 22) ISBN 089941978X.

Lewis, M.K., and Rosemary R. Lewis. Your Film Acting Career: How to Break into the Movies and TV and Survive in Hollywood. 4th ed., rev. and updated. Gorham House, 1997. 320p. index. $16.95 pap. ISBN 0929149025.
Covers a wide range of topics of concern to would-be actors: finding work in television, films, commercials, industrials, new media, modeling, student films, theatre, etc.; living in the Los Angeles area; developing effective resumes and photographs; joining unions; obtaining an agent; what producers, directors and casting directors look for in interviews, cold readings and on the set; sele cting acting classes; legal considerations such as residuals, overtime, contracts, etc.; and restarting a stalled career.

Liff, Alvin A., and others. Color and Black & White Television Theory and Servicing. 3rd ed. Prentice-Hall College Division, 1993. 592p. il. $97.00. ISBN 0131500120.
Outlines the essentials of TV repair, from black-and-white and color receivers to video tape recorder theory and practice. Coverage includes cable, pay, and satellite television systems, microcomputer-controlled remote control systems, and triggered and dual trace oscilloscopes. Geared specifically to electronics technicians concerned with TV troubleshooting.

Miller, Lisa Anne, and Mark Northam. Film and Television Composer's Resource Guide: The Complete Guide to Organizing and Building Your Business. Spiral ed. Hal Leonard Publishing Corporation, 1998. 198p. $34.95 pap. ISBN 0793595614.

Robin, Michael, with Michael Poulin. Digital Television Fundamentals: Design and Installation of Video and Audio Systems. New York: McGraw-Hill, 1997. 550p. McGraw-Hill Video/Audio Engineering Series) $60.00. ISBN 0070531684. Geared to assisting broadcast engineers in the transition from analog to digital television. Includes guidelines for assuring equipment compatibility in analog, digital, or mixed systems, meeting relevant standards requirements, and measuring performance in audio and video equipment. Covers data multiplexing, JPEG and MPEG compression schemes, signal processing, and multimedia.

Sawyer, Tom, with Arthur David Weingarten. Plots Unlimited: For the Writer of Novels, Short Stories, Plays, Screenplays and Television Episodes: A Creative Source for Generating a Virtually Limitless Number and Variety of Story Plots and Outlines. Ashleywilde, Inc., 1995. 296p. $25.00 pap. ISBN 0962747602. Based on an award-winning computer software program, the book serve as a thesaurus of plot developments--5,600 in all (with over 200,000 permutations possible). It covers virtually every aspect of human relationships in focusing on that essential element of both comedy and drama, conflict. Sawyer--formerly Head Writer/Producer of *Murder, She Wrote* and its spinoff series, *The Law & Harry McGraw*--has written many TV pilots and network teleplays and is the co- librettist/lyricist of the opera, *Jack*.

Silver, David. How to Pitch & Sell Your TV Script. Writers Digest Books, 1991. 162p. $17.95. ISBN 0898794676.

Stephens, Mitchell. Broadcast News. 3rd ed. HBJ College & School Division, 1997. $54.50. ISBN 0030791766. A thorough, well- written primer on radio and television journalism. The *New York Times* considers this to be the most widely used--at institutions of higher learning-- introduction of its kind.

Stephenson, D.J. Newnes. Guides to Satellite TV: Installation, Reception and Repair. 4th ed. Butterworth-Heinemann, 1997. 383p. $42.95. ISBN 0750634758.

Straczynski, J. Michael. The Complete Book of Scriptwriting. Rev ed. Writers Digest Books, 1996. 424p. $22.99. ISBN 0898795125. As a general introduction to writing for television, film, radio, animation, and stage, this work by a working writer/producer is without peer. Updates the original 1981 edition in areas such as fluctuating markets, the CD-ROM format, and recent Writers' Guild strikes.

Utterback, Ann S. Broadcast Voice Handbook: How to Polish Your On-Air Delivery. 2nd ed. Bonus Books, 1995. $29.95. ISBN 1566250226. Widely considered the classic manual for broadcast methodology. Employs a practical, down-to-earth approach likely to work with students and beginning professionals as well as to experienced on-air personnel.

Utterback, Ann S. Broadcaster's Survival Guide: Staying Alive in the Business. Bonus Books, 1997. 170p. bibl. $24.95 pap. ISBN 1566250927.

Provides techniques to assist news directors, producers, station general managers, on air talent, and other news professionals in recognizing stresses and dealing with them in healthy ways. Utterback has also included a listing of resources which will enable broadcasting personnel to obtain additional help.

Walter, Richard. Screenwriting: The Art, Craft, and Business of Film and Television. Reissue ed. New American Library, 1992. $13.95 pap. ISBN 0452263476. Walter, affiliated with the UCLA Screenwriting Program, provides guidelines to creating, reworking, and marketing screenplays. Whereas Syd Field--in *The Screenwriter's Problem Solver: How to Recognize, Identify, and Define Screenwriting Problems*--focuses on ground rules regarding overall structure and plot points, Walter stimulates the reader to get involved with the writing process.

Weaver, Dan, and Jason Siegel. Breaking into Television: Proven Advice from Veterans and Interns. Petersons Guides, 1998. 254p. $14.95 pap. ISBN 0768901219. This tool lives up to its billing as the "only book that brings a career in television into focus." It provides insights and advice from more than 100 seasoned TV executives-- e.g., the Programming Chief of MTV, a producer from *The Today Show*, a marketing executive from Disney, an associate producer from *Oprah*--all of whom started out as interns. Includes appendices with internship opportunities.

Wharton, Brooke A. The Writer Got Screwed (But Didn't Have To): A Guide to the Legal and Business Practices of Writing for the Entertainment Industry. New York: HarperCollins, 1996. 288p. $22.00. ISBN 0062701304. Wharton has produced a valuable companion to multitude of writing guides presently available. Covers business law and ethics relating to the contractual arrangements between screenwriters and agents, media firms, etc.

Whitaker, Jerry. DTV: The Revolution In Electronic Imaging. New York: McGraw-Hill, 1998. 400p. $55.00. ISBN 0070696268. Delineates the recently developed standards relating to digital television; DTV is presently merging telecommunications, broadcasting, and computers into a video information vehicle likely to revolutionize culture worldwide. The work should prove particularly useful to broadcast and video engineers for its coverage of transmission and reception hardware, the operating principles of the forthcoming U.S. video transmission/interchange format, attributes of video images that allow signal prediction, and video compression technology.

White, Ted. Broadcast News Writing, Reporting, and Producing. 2nd ed. 408p. Focal Press, April 1996. $39.95. ISBN 0240802454. An exhaustive compendium of broadcast journalism methods. Eight of the twentythree chapters concentrate on the basics of broadcast news, from general skills to specialty reporting to ethics. Includes script samples from famous journalists such as Edward R. Murrow, Charles Kuralt, Walter Cronkite, Eric Sevareid, and Charles Osgood; they also discuss how they write and report. The work emphasizes real- life situations; everyday problems faced by reporters, writers, assignment editors, and producers are covered as well as such topics as investigative reporting, the job market, legal issues, and interviewing techniques. Each chapter incoporates exercises for writing, review, and discussion in order that students have the opportunity to apply what they've read.

Woodbridge, Patricia. Scenic Drafting for Theatre, Film & Television Principles & Professional Examples. Drama Publishers, 1999. Price information not available. pap. ISBN 0896761452.
Woodbridge presents the basics of scenic drafting for students and beginning professionals. The text is augmented by the selective use of practice-based models.

Yorke, Ivor. Basic TV Reporting. 2nd ed. Butterworth-Heinemann, 1997. 168p. $24.95. ISBN 0240514343.
A practice-based primer on broadcast journalism. While the work is probably overly simplistic for seasoned television news personnel, it should be useful to anyone seeking insights into the techniques of the profession.

SPECIAL COLLECTIONS--FILM INDUSTRY

American Film Institute. c/o Anne G. Schlosser, Director. Louis B. Mayer Library, P.O. Box 27999, 2021 N. Western Avenue, Los Angeles, CA 90027. (213) 856-7655. Accessibility: Open to the public.
The Script Collection includes thousands of film and television scripts, many of which were working copies for directors, writers, editors, and script supervisors. The MGM Script Collection encompasses 400 scripts from the silent period up to the mid-1950s. The Columbia Pictures Stills Collection covers the period 1930-1950. The Oral History Program Collection has interviews with pioneers of the industry as well as transcripts of AFI seminars. A film production and file index provides documentation on nearly all U.S. films from 1930 to 1969; each title is tracked from the first trade announcement regarding film production to its final release.

National Film, Television and Sound Archives. Documentation & Public Services, 395 Wellington St., Ottawa, K1A 0N3, Canada.
Comprised of several collections including 1060 periodical titles (450 current), 265,000 picture-stills, 6,000 posters, and extensive microfiche holdings.

National Museum of Communications & Library. 6305 N. O'Connor, Suite 123, Irving, TX 75039. (214) 690-3636.
The library--comprising more than 30,000 volumes--includes books, films, video and audio recordings devoted to the mass media, most notably the cinema and television.

Sherman Grinberg Film Libraries, Inc. c/o Bill Brewington, 1040 N. McCadden Place, Hollywood, CA 90038-3787. (213) 464-7491. New York Office: Nancy Casey, 630 Ninth Avenue, New York, NY 10036-3787. (212) 765-5170. Accessibility: Monday-Friday, 9:30-5:30. Scholars, public. fees: $25 per hour, $50 minimum; includes viewing, research, and computer printouts.

This is the largest known news and stock footage film and tape library covering the twentieth century. Its resources include footage from ABC News (1963-present), Pathe News (1989-1957), Paramount News (1926-1957), MGM features and television stock footage, *Nova* and *Odyssey* television stock footage, selected BBC programming, Fitzpatrick Short Subjects, etc.

University of Iowa. Special Collections & University Archives, Iowa City, Iowa 52242. (319) 335-5921.
The archive consists of ten notable collections: Robert Blees Collection of motion picture and television material, 1925-65--stories, still production photos, motion picture and television scripts; David Swift Collection of motion picture and television material, 1951-65--scripts, posters, photos, drawings, and blueprints; Alber Jay Cohen Collection of motion picture and television production material, 1948-58--correspondence, film scripts, stories, photos, financial and production papers, and censorship records; Arthur A. Ross Collection of motion picture and television material, 1943-65--correspondence, scripts, photos, production records, and artists' sketches; Norman Felton Collection of papers, 1937-78; Ralph M. Junkin Collection- film stills (mostly from silent era), lobby posters, window cards, display posters, pressbook materials, etc.; Nicholas Meyer Collection--papers of a leading screenwriter and director; Stewart Stern Collection-- papers of a film and television writer; Twentieth Century-Fox Script Collection--script material on nearly 1,400 titles from 1929-1969; Richard Malbaum Collection-- playscripts, drafts, treatments and various versions of screenplays, teleplay scripts, notes, correspondence, reviews, research materials, photographs, photographs, and memorabilia.

Walt Disney Archives. c/o David R. Smith, Archivist. 500 S. Buena Vista Street, Burbank, CA 91521. (818) 840-5424. Accessibility: Monday-Friday, 8-5. Scholars, public. Advance appointment and specific research projects required.
The definitive Disney archive, including the founder's office correspondence files (1930-1966) and assorted earlier files, in addition to personal memorabilia, recordings and transcripts of speeches, awards, 8,000 photographs of Disney, a Disney family history, and a collection of miniatures. Also present are about 1,000 Disney books published in the United States, a representative collection of Disney books published in thirty-five languages, a complete run of domestic Disney comic books and most foreign comics (1932-present), a nearly complete collection of phonograph records issued by the Walt Disney Music Company, several hundred singles and albums of Disney songs issued by other recording companies, tape recordings, sheet music of Disney titles, a vast clippings file dating from 1924, over 500,000 negatives of photographs related to Disney and his enterprises, thousands of Disney toys and memorabilia, copies of Disney films (along with scripts, cutting continuities, and other production information), a large collection of movie props and artifacts, data covering the history of Disney theme parks and Audio-Animatronics, most of Disney's original artwork, and oral histories of Disney conducted with his key employees. All resources are organized, with key materials fully indexed.

SPECIAL COLLECTIONS--TELEVISION

Library of Congress. Motion Picture, Broadcasting and Recorded Sound Division, Washington, D.C. 20540. (202) 707-5840. Fax: (202) 707-2371.
The extensive holdings include the *Amateur Hour* and *Arthur Godfrey Time* collections. The former features disc, tape, and television coverage of the Ted Mack series (1948-1969), including applications for program appearances and news clippings; the latter is comprised of recordings of the television and radio broadcasts from 1949-1957, along with selected rehearsals and warm-ups.

Los Angeles Public Library. Frances Howard Goldwyn Hollywood Regional Library, 1623 Ivar Ave., Los Angeles, CA 90028. (213) 467-2821. Fax: (213) 467-5707.
The general and research archive is comprised of more than 100,000 items--manuscripts, pictures, scripts, production materials, papers, correspondence, vertical file resources, etc.--covering the cinema, radio, and television. Special collections include Rod Warren, Russell S. Hughes, and J.H. Peyser.

Museum of Television and Radio Library. 25 W. 52nd St., New York, NY 10019. (212) 752-4690.
Geared to the study and preservation of radio and television broadcasting history, the institution administers a collection of notable programming (over 20,000 separate shows) as well as books and original scripts.

National Broadcasting Company. c/o Vera Mayer. Vice President, Information and Archives Reference Library, 30 Rockefeller Plaza, Room 1426, New York, NY 10020.
The collection--comprising monographs, periodicals, clippings, microforms, and other formats--documents the entire history of the medium as well as related topics, such as business, politics, and social issues.

New York Public Library. c/o Dorothy L. Swerdlove, Curator. Billy Rose Theatre Collection, Performing Arts Research Center, 111 Amsterdam Avenue, New York, NY 10023.
Since 1941, it has been the official repository of the American Tele vision Society. The holdings include clipping files on radio and television programs and their respective personnel; photographs of these individuals, of radio and television studios, equipment, etc.; television production scripts (most notably, most of the *Hallmark Hall of Fame* specials and *Studio One* scripts); radio scripts; and monographs devoted to the history of broadcasting and telecasting and the techniques of the industry.

Popular Culture Archive. Bowling Green State University, Bowling Green, OH 43403. E-mail: bmccall@opie.bgsu.edu.
Includes more than 400 linear feet of TV scripts for soap operas (dating back as far as 1954), production documentation, and commercial materials donated by the Proctor and Gamble Company.

Smithsonian Institution Libraries. National Museum of American History Branch, Washington, D.C. 20560.
Holdings feature Allen Balcom DuMont's work, particularly after the institution of DuMont Laboratories, Inc. to manufacture cathode ray tubes and television receivers.

Television Information Office. 745 Fifth Ave., New York, NY 10022.
Focuses on the social and cultural aspects of the medium. Resources include research studies, serials, clipping and pamphlet files, books, and government publications.

University of California, Los Angeles. Arts, Architecture & Urban Planning Library, Special Collections 22478 University Research Library, Los Angeles, CA 90024. (310) 825-7253. Fax: (310) 206-3374. E-mail: ecz5tha@mvs.oac.ucla.edu.
Built around more than 200 collections culled from the studio holdings of Twentieth Century-Fox Film Corporation, RKO, Columbia, Paramount, and MGM, among others. Includes primary source materials such as motion picture stills (4,000,000+), scripts, production files, and personal papers and professional archives of actors, directors, producers, art directors, and writers. These resources are augmented by clipping files, posters, lobbycards, and original sketches.

University of Oregon Library. Special Collections Division, Eugene, OR 97403.
Comprised of more than twenty manuscript collections featuring television scripts and some production materials for westerns (e.g., *Gunsmoke*, *Bonanza*, *Wagon Train*), mystery, and adventure shows.

University of Pennsylvania. Annenberg School for Communication Library, 3620 Walnut St., Philadelphia, PA 19104-6220. (215) 898-7027. Fax: 215-898-2024.
Features almost 3,000 television scripts from prime-time network series. Accessible via an index.

YEARBOOKS AND ANNUALS--TELEVISION

Lovece, Frank. The Television Yearbook: Complete, Detailed Listings for the 1990-1991 Season. New York: Perigee Books/Putnam, 1992. 271p. $16.95 pap. ISBN 0-399-51702-2.
The tool includes every prime-time network television comedy, drama, or variety series--as well as notable cable station and syndicated programs, arranged alphabetically by title. The entries cite network, series description, regular cast, and an itemized listing of episodes which notes episode title, plot synopsis, cast members, writers, directors, and broadcast date (along with preemptions and last- minute cast changes). Appended by inventory of unsold programs, both those aired and those unscheduled for air time.

Printed in Great Britain
by Amazon.co.uk, Ltd.,
Marston Gate.